PIGSTIES AND PARADISE:
Lady Diarists and the Tour of Wales
1795 – 1860

Pigsties and Paradise:
Lady Diarists and the Tour of Wales
1795 – 1860

Liz Pitman

Published with the financial support
of the Welsh Books Council

ISBN: 978-1-84527-249-4

Cover design: Sian Parri

First published in 2009 by
Gwasg Carreg Gwalch
12 Iard yr Orsaf, Llanrwst, Wales LL26 0EH
tel: 01492 624031
fax: 01492 641502
email: books@carreg-gwalch.com
website: www.carreg-gwalch.com

For David

Contents

Acknowledgements

I am grateful to those archivists listed below in whose record offices the diaries included in this book were found. Extracts from the diaries have, in all cases, been made with their kind permission.

Bedfordshire & Luton Archives
& Record Service (BLARS)

British Library
Caernarfon Record Office
Cardiff Libraries and
Information Service

Dorset History Centre
Essex Record Office
Gloucestershire Record Office

Hampshire Record Office
Library, Amgueddfa Cymru/
National Museum Wales
Llyfrgell Genedlaethol Cymru/
National Library of Wales
Shropshire Records and
Research Centre
Wigan Services Archives
(WLCT)
Worcestershire Record Office

Ann Bletchley,
Frederica Rouse Boughton
Frances Anne Crewe
Harriet Alderson

Judith Beecroft, Annie Hodgson,
Charlotte Skinner, Esther Williams
Elizabeth Bower
Millicent Bant
Mary Anne and Sarah Hibbert,
Mary Russell
Margaret Martineau

Sarah Wilmot (Haslam)

Ann Atherton

Louisa Charlotte Kenyon

Sarah Haslam (Wilmot)
Ann Porter

I am also particularly grateful to the Bedfordshire and Luton Archives and Record Service (BLARS) for their permission to include the paintings done by Frederica Rouse Boughton; National Museum of Wales for those by Sarah Wilmot, and Wigan Archives Service, WLCT, for those also done by Sarah Wilmot (neé Haslam, under which name her diary in Wigan is listed).

Archivists are, in my experience, the most helpful and enthusiastic of people, and I am very appreciative of the assistance given by all those who helped with the many questions I had arising from the content of the diaries. In particular I would like to thank Alan Davies, archivist, Wigan Archives Service; James Collett-White, archivist, Bedfordshire and Luton Archives and Record Service, and John Kenyon, Librarian, Library, Amgueddfa Genedlaethol Cymru – National Museum Wales, all of whom gave me considerable help with the diaries found in their archives and used in this book.

Thanks also go to Ann Bryan for her help with aspects of the Welsh language; the Cambrian Archaeological Association, who made a generous grant towards the original research; Jane Jenkins for her generous support, both practical and financial; as well as those publicans and others who have helped with general information. My thanks also go to Sheelagh Moreton, Lord Raglan, Sue and Richard Skinner, and Malcolm Thomas, all of whom read earlier drafts and made helpful comments; Margaret Howl for help with proof-reading, and Simon Bradshaw, my computer troubleshooter. Specific thanks are due as follows:

Chapter 1:
Jack Calow (Picturesque Society): the Picturesque
Major H. Porter: permission to use extracts from Anne Porter's diary

Chapter 2:
Mike Beales of the Castell Malgwyn hotel: history of the Sir Benjamin Hammett's Penygored Tin Works
Paul Cattini: information on Caldey Island
Tenby Museum: bathing habits in Tenby
Sir Michael Wilmot Bt.: generous help with the family tree of his forebear, John Wilmot

Chapter 3:
Bersham Heritage Museum: John Wilkinson
FSC Orielton: Orielton and Stack Rocks
Greenwich Heritage Centre: Lady Wilson
Pontypridd Museum: Berw Taff

Chapter 4:
Andrew Richards: Richards family tree, and photographs of Caerynwch and the Torrent Walk
Nick Steele of Melbourne, Australia and Alyson Wilson of the Clapham Society: both alerted me to the extensive wider family archive

Chapter 5:
Professor Robert Pearce: Lampeter College
Peter Welford: Gwydir Castle

Chapter 6:
Huyshe Bower: permission to use Elizabeth Bower's diary

Chapter 7:
Vaughan Gaskell: Nannau
Michael Orlebar, great-grandson of Frederica Rouse Boughton: for permission to use both her written diary and the watercolours contained in it

Finally, particular thanks go to three people - Michael Freeman, curator, Ceredigion Museum in Aberystwyth, who was extremely helpful with some of the background research; Jen Llywelyn of Gwasg Carreg Gwalch for her encouragement and skilled editing; and in particular my friend David Barnes, whose friendship and support enabled this book to be written.

My hope is that other Welsh travel diaries, whether in private hands or the public domain, will be uncovered as a result of my own research. Although I have done extensive checking of the information in the book it has not always been possible, even with the sterling help of local archivists, to find answers to all my questions. The diarists themselves, since they were not writing with a view to posterity, often give only tantalisingly brief or non-existent information about questions that arose from my reading – questions such as: 'What kinds of boots did they wear for climbing Snowdon (*Yr Wyddfa*)?'; 'Did they always take their maids?'; and 'What was the flesh and blood monument at Llantrisant?' (chapter 3) I would be grateful for any information on these unanswered questions.

Any mistakes that remain in the text are entirely my responsibility.

Foreword

This book is the result of research into little-known unpublished diaries of women travellers to Wales in the latter half of the eighteenth and beginning of the nineteenth centuries. The 'picturesque' was a new fashion; these intrepid women were seeking it, and while doing so they left us a lively account of these early days of tourism. Travelling over rough roads and staying in inns which sometimes seemed as grubby as pigsties, they found a paradise in the landscape and antiquities of the countryside.

There was Frances Crewe, sometime lover of Sheridan; serious Sarah Wilmot, wife of an MP; the autocratic Lady Wilson and her faithful companion, Millicent, who kept the diary. Then there was Mary Anne Hibbert, who, despite falling into one gentleman's arms and setting her cap at another, never married. She was always dogged by disaster on her travels, but she returned to Wales on several occasions, climbing Snowdon (at the age of 59), as did the much younger honeymooner, Elizabeth Bower. There was Margaret Martineau, who travelled with a gang of cousins and an uncle, whilst the wonderful Frederica Rouse Boughton, whose watercolours are a delight, waxed lyrical about the area around Dolgellau, which she explored by pony cart and on horseback with her sisters and some friends.

These women were endlessly curious, and they wrote with honesty and humour about all that they saw. This makes their accounts more interesting, perceptive and fun than most of the male diarists of the period. They were stoical when things went wrong; when they got lost they admitted to it, and when they were soaked to the skin, they shared their discomfort, though often in an amusing way as befits adventures in a strange land.

Liz Pitman has made a selection from these fascinating accounts, bringing out the women's voices clearly while weaving them together to make an informative and entertaining read.

Raglan.

Lord Raglan

The Discovery

Journal of a twelve weeks tour: It has been ask'd what is the use of writing Journals?
I answer, various: some who have talent write for the vanity that others may read &
commend their cleverness. Others, to prove that they can observe as well as see. Some
(of whom I number one) with a view to improvement; to mark the degree of happiness
each spot afforded in the society of those who are dear to them and to impress the
beauties of Art & Nature more strongly on the memory.
Sarah Wilmot, 1st August 1795

* * *

Travelling for pleasure has a long history. From Tudor times the wealthy, educated man (and occasional woman) undertook the Grand Tour of Europe; whilst the really adventurous traveller explored far-flung exotic places in other parts of the world. Travelling in Britain was, until the middle of the eighteenth century, not something that the sophisticated tourist did but as the century wore on, some curious travellers began to discover their own country. When I began this research I was living in Wales and I was curious to know more about early tourism in this small but beautiful country for, although Wales was not a popular destination for the earliest of the travellers for pleasure, it had, by the late eighteenth century, become popular with the 'picturesque' tourist. Many of these early tourists published their travel diaries, but the majority were by men, with well over a hundred being published in the late eighteenth and early nineteenth centuries. By contrast only a handful of women's Welsh travel diaries were published. Yet I had a hunch that many more women travellers must have written diaries, a hunch that was confirmed when I found in *The Observant Traveller* that there were at least eighty such unpublished Welsh diaries in record offices up and down the country.

Having decided to find out more about them, I always arrived with a sense of excitement at a record office where I knew a diary to be held and, whenever a 'new' diary arrived on my table, and I had adjusted my eyes to the faded, spidery or bold handwriting, I held my breath, wondering whether the diary would be an interesting one or merely a list of places visited. I was rarely disappointed, for these women, rattling into Wales in stuffy carriages on poor roads, staying in inns that they sometimes shared with fleas and rats, and climbing the Welsh mountains in long skirts, nevertheless found time to write with animated feeling about their experiences.

I soon realised that, in turning the original research into a book, I had to set some geographical and time boundaries. Although there are some diaries dating from the 1770s, these have not been included because, with one exception, they are too brief to be of interest. The exception is the lively diary written by Jinny Jenks in 1772, but her diary, fascinating though it is, is mainly an account of the grand houses she stayed in when visiting the Vale of Clwyd.[1] The time span chosen, therefore, was from 1795 – when travellers began to visit Wales in considerable numbers – and 1860 when, with the coming of the train, travel became easier and not just for the privileged few.

Deciding how to condense the vast amount of material I had into a book was also a daunting task but, as I read the diaries, the personalities of some of the writers in particular began to emerge from the pages, and I found myself in the company of women who were sometimes prejudiced, but always lively and interesting. I therefore decided on a 'person' approach, and the book is based on those diaries where I have been able to find out at least a little about the writer, and where I feel their character shines through their writing.

These diarists were often overwhelmed by Welsh generosity and hospitality, but they could be irritated by what they felt was indifferent service and amused by local customs. In the countryside they often felt that they had arrived in paradise, but they were quick to criticise those towns and inns that they felt were like 'pigsties'. Sadly, as the diarists were presumably not expecting later generations to be curious about their stories, they nearly always miss out things that we would find interesting but were, perhaps, commonplace for them – what they wore, for example, for climbing mountains; how much they planned their travels; whether they sent letters of introduction ahead; how they paid their way, and so on. Yet despite this, two hundred or so years after they were written, these diaries still provide a fascinating glimpse into life in late eighteenth- and early nineteenth-century Wales.

This book has several aims. The first is to bring some interesting, but generally unknown, historical material by women to public awareness. Secondly, it will help to redress the balance between published male and female travel diarists of the period. Thirdly, it can act as a gazetteer for today's tourists of the journeys of the period, most of which followed a set route based on passable roads and available inns. As most of the places visited by the tourists can still be seen, they appear in **bold** type when they are first mentioned in the text. Appendix 2 provides information about their present-day status, whilst maps show the routes undertaken. Finally, it is intended to be an enjoyable book which gives present-day readers a glimpse of both the joys and hazards of early tourism.

One of the strengths of these diaries is that their authors wrote down exactly what they felt about what they saw and, as a result, they have a 'warts and all' feel about them, as they have not been edited for what we might nowadays think of as 'political correctness'. The book is based on extensive extracts from the diaries, with my comments merely adding factual information that will, I hope, help a modern reader to make greater sense of these women's adventures. It does not intend to be an analysis, from a twenty-first century viewpoint, of nineteenth-century attitudes, but simply to be an enjoyable and interesting perspective on a fascinating period in Welsh history. I have generally used the present tense in order to keep the 'here and now' flavour of the diaries. I have also kept the idiosyncratic spelling used by the diarists, so that apparent typographical 'mistakes' in the quotations from the diaries are simply the original spelling. I have, however, occasionally amended punctuation so that the extracts make grammatical sense.

Chapter 1

Women Travellers, Wales and the Picturesque

After resting and amusing ourselves for an hour on the summit, we began the work of going down, far more difficult and unpleasant than going up . . . the abominable steep and craggy path . . . turns your head and gives you a sensation (for in reality nothing can be safer than you are on your sure-footed pony) that you are doing something very perilous. It was very amusing as well as satisfactory to see how those patient creatures picked their steps between the immense stones, amounting to rocks, of which the path is full.

Ann Atherton, describing her descent of **Snowdon**, 1st October 1825

* * *

The wildness of the Welsh landscape for these women, who mainly came from English cities or the gentle English countryside, would have seemed awe-inspiring indeed, and their diaries are full of excited descriptions of mountains and waterfalls, as well as people who seemed exotic, with their strange customs, costumes and language. And, to add to their vivid written descriptions, the diarists often sketched what they saw, often in far from ideal conditions. When Mary Anne Hibbert sets out to sketch in 1856 she finds that 'nothing is perfect . . . we were plagued with wasps as well as pigs, geese and other animals, however I staid out drawing as long as my eyes would serve . . . and walked till my legs also were done up when I was obliged to come in to be idle'. When it rained, and a closed carriage made it impossible to see the landscape, the diarists simply used their imagination to describe what they thought they ought to be seeing, as does a testy sounding Louisa Charlotte Kenyon when dashing through the **Llanberis Pass**:

> ... never was there a more lovely view & what a fine effect of light & shade would doubtless have been displayed with my hard metallic pencil! had not a cruel shower of rain obliged me to shut the book & alas! alas! I am now writing with the carriage shut up, & we are descending the pass of Llanberis without seeing anything of the grand forms of the grandest mountains in Wales . . . I suspect that our imaginations assist in showing us the very finest, the grandest, the sublimest scene possible. (*23rd May 1839*)

The diarists were also great 'people watchers'. Unlike today's 'kiss and tell' writers, they were discreet about their private lives, but there were still moments when ladies 'fell into gentlemen's arms', maids were kissed, or inebriated landlords 'mistook' the room of one of their women guests for their own. Wry comments were also made about fellow travellers. Anne Porter, staying at the **Castle Inn** in **Brecon** (*Aberhonddu*) is highly amused by a newly married couple. The wife 'was what they called a great Welsh heiress . . . she was rather pretty but is out of health & looked much too frightened to eat. Her husband, un Médicin, is disagreeable looking & I think too old for her & doesn't look 'amoureux' of the lady'. The next person to catch her eye is a 'wife to a rich Welsh squire who, with her daughters, was dashing about the town. She is a great huntress which is very much the fashion with the Welsh ladies who sometimes turn out with the hounds 14 or 15 in number'.

Although these women diarists never journeyed to Wales alone, but travelled with husbands, uncles, sisters or friends and, in some cases, coachmen and servants, they were, nevertheless, intrepid women. Their everyday world was that of the gentry or the affluent middle class. They ran large homes, went to balls and card parties, and enjoyed genteel activities such as reading and sketching. They performed 'good works', visited the poor, established almshouses, set up societies for orphans and went frequently to church. None of them had careers, as we know them today, but they were nevertheless educated and cultured and living at a time when the traditional role of women was being challenged. As early as 1795 Mrs Mary Morgan, one of the few women to publish an account of her travels, was spiritedly addressing those men 'who think a woman cannot find leisure to write, without neglecting either her person or some part of her family duty'; or that women were 'formed merely to dress and be admired, or for domestic drudgery'. Firmly she tells them that 'those notions have long ago been exploded by people of polite manners and liberal education'.

The early tourists in Britain seldom ventured to Wales for it was, until the eighteenth century, regarded as a wild, foreign place, with a mainly peasant population, who were said to eat toasted cheese because they couldn't afford meat. Attitudes began to change with the development of the Picturesque Movement. The Revd William Gilpin had argued that Edmund Burke's two aesthetic categories of the 'sublime', seen in awesome sights such as great mountains; and the 'beautiful', found in peaceful, pretty sights, were insufficient; his use of the word 'picturesque' became a third category to describe 'wild' or 'irregular' elements in the landscape.

And so, as the eighteenth century wore on, more and more enthusiastic tourists set out in their carriages to explore this 'picturesque' landscape, as well as the antiquities and the burgeoning industry of Wales. They carried with them not only their diaries and sketch pads, but their trusty guidebooks. The first was Gilpin's *Observations*, which told them how to look at the landscape in 'picturesque' terms. The second was the great Welsh travel writer Thomas Pennant's *Tour of Wales (1784)*, which told discerning travellers which antiquities they should admire.

This increase in tourism was also aided when the French Revolution began in 1789, for travelling to Europe on the Grand Tour lost something of its appeal when it meant passing through a country where people's heads were being cut off. War abroad and, at times, near famine at home meant that the fear of a home-grown revolution by the poor and dispossessed was very real, a fear that made people quake in their shoes and sometimes in their beds, as does Ann Bletchley when she stays at the **Angel Inn** in **Abergavenny** *(Y Fenni)* in 1812. She finds that there is a French officer in the bedroom next to hers and is terrified, for as the rooms are so similar:

> . . . nothing seemed more likely than to mistake one for the other and of course we were anxious to secure the door but to our great disappointment found that so far from having lock or bolt it would not even latch. To remedy this evil we attempted to form a barricade with our trunk but alas! this had been already made use of by the chambermaid to secure us from the rats who had gained access to this room. A little more contrivance overcame this difficulty also and notwithstanding our discomfort we sunk to sleep even though our enemy was close at our side . . . the number of French prisoners in the town whose appearance was really miserable gave us . . . a great aversion to the place which is otherwise neat and agreeable. *(undated letter)*

By the time Frederica Rouse Boughton travelled to Wales in 1860, Victoria had been queen for twenty-three years of her long reign, and Britain was an industrial society, as well as a dominant world power with an Empire stretching into the far corners of the world. In Wales the Industrial Revolution gathered pace when its mineral wealth of coal, copper and iron began to be exploited. Small towns such as **Merthyr Tydfil, Newport, Swansea and Cardiff** *(Merthyr Tudful, Casnewydd, Abertawe and Caerdydd)* grew rapidly into sprawling, teeming, unsanitary centres of industry. Swansea, for example, once a pleasant sea bathing town, had, so the widow Judith Beecroft reports, by 1827, 'rows of high chimneys belching forth flame & smoke' and 'copper, iron, brass and tin works . . . which have so impregnated the air with smoke that every lane and road is blackened'. Yet, although a few travellers were appalled by what they saw, most were entranced. In 1836 Esther Williams visits the iron works at **Maesteg** and, when it is dark, she watches:

> . . . the tapping of the furnace, when the red hot liquid iron is let off into places prepared for it. This was indeed a wonderful sight . . . it is the business of one man to direct the liquid stream (by means of a long pole) to the several partitions ready for it, when it quickly cools and forms long bars, which are called pig iron. We were much pleased with this novel sight, as novel as it was wonderful, to see iron in a liquid state, running red hot from the furnace, and soon cooling, a quantity of sand being thrown over it. *(19th July 1836)*

Nearly twenty years later, in 1855, Annie Hodgson is equally entranced by

Penrhyn slate quarries, although her factual description is mixed up with a gossiping one. As she stands on a nearby hillside and looks down into the quarry she sees:

> . . . all around and far below was a busy scene of men working. Some were suspended by ropes with their feet on pieces of wood, cutting and hammering at the slate . . . when at 9 o'clock a man from the highest point of the highest hill sounded a bugle to warn the men to go to their little slate cabins which are scattered about. Presently another bugle note is sounded and the workmen hurry away as fast as possible to the huts, and not a creature is to be seen outside. Then the blasting begins and the booming sound reverberates round & round the large & deep amphitheatre as one burst and another issues from the rocks, bringing masses of the stone away. The heir [to all this] . . . I very unwittingly came upon as he was kissing the maid of the hotel upon the top of the stairs . . . there are three resident surgeons as accidents happen every day, & sometimes very serious they are. *(16th November 1855)*

Engineering marvels such as road, bridge and aqueduct building also excited the minds of the diarists. Telford's **Menai Bridge** was seen, when it opened in 1826, as one of the wonders of the modern world, for it reduced the travel time from London to Holyhead from thirty-six to twenty-seven hours. Ann Atherton, walking across it shortly before it was opened, sounds both excited and frightened, when she reports:

> [I] walked across the bridge & back, but not without giddiness & a feeling of danger, with nothing between you & the sea a hundred feet below you, but apparently slender bars of iron, & loose planks laid over them amongst which there are everywhere openings through which you see the water, & which sway as you tread upon them, no balustrade at present except slender iron uprights with long intervals between them'. *(28th September 1825)*

Despite this rapid industrialisation and urbanisation, food shortages and the enclosures of common land still meant that the life of the average Welsh farm worker was often wretched. Although the diarists were amused by things they found strange or exotic, they seemed genuine in their concern for the poverty they saw, as does Harriet Alderson when she and her fellow travellers stop at a cottage in north Wales to request a crust of bread. They find that:

> . . . the woman belonging to the cottage . . . did not understand a word of English . . . [but] she placed before us whatever her humble cot could afford viz. wheaten bread, barley bread, oat cakes, cheese, butter, honey, mead, milk & water. The house had only one small

window in it so that we could hardly distinguish from one end of it to the other. The floor was the bare earth, & the walls had no plastering or whitewash, but were merely the rough stone of which the cottage was built. A few sticks were blazing in the hearth or rather mud floor over which was suspended a large saucepan, full of potatoes. There was a large open chimney to let out the smoke. The candle which the woman lighted to fetch the milk from a dark corner, was a rush twisted and dipt in grease. Such is a picture of a Welsh peasant, considered to be in good circumstances. What would our labourers say to such an abode? *(September 1818)*

Yet despite this poverty the diarists clearly saw that, however poor they might be:

the Peasantry are very proud, in the humblest dwelling you will see china plates & cups & saucers ranged on shelves & if there is a second room, then the . . . corner cupboard is grandly set forth. We asked them if they would not like to wear bonnets instead of beaver hats. "No, no was the reply not if you gave us ever so much". The gown she had on, had lasted 12 years, of wool & cotton of their own weaving . . . it is the regular dress of the country, warm & substantial'. *(Judith Beecroft, 30th June 1827)*

Two major outcomes of the discontent that grew out of poverty and harsh living and working conditions were a zeal for education and a massive growth in religious non-conformity. When Esther Williams visits a school she finds it:

. . . to contain between 2 and 3 hundred persons. The school is especially for the work people, and here they are taught to read. It was a gratifying sight to see so many people of all ages met together to be instructed. Mr. Smith senr. gave out some Welsh hymns which they sang remarkably well. All the people were remarkably clean and respectable in their dress and the contrast was so great that we could hardly believe that many of them were really the same as we had seen and pitied the preceding day, then so squalid and dirty – now a pattern of neatness and cleanliness. *(23rd July 1836)*

As for religion, the Anglican Church in Wales had become increasingly out of touch with the needs of its Welsh congregation; many of the clergy were Englishmen who were seldom to be seen in the parish, or Welshmen who were often very poor. With parishioners left spiritually, as well as physically, hungry, various non-conformist denominations, such as Methodism, took root and flourished. Charlotte Skinner, on a visit to mid-Wales describes how the Methodists had pitched a tent in a local field, remaining there for three days and:

> . . . preaching I believe from break of day to sunset. There were numerous preachers who drew to the spot an immense concourse of devoted hearers. This sect is very prevalent in Wales; I observed a meeting house in almost every village . . . I was not near enough to hear in what language these preachers were holding forth; their vociferation, audible at some distance, fully satisfied my curiosity. *(July 1808)*

As well as religious non-conformity, the prevalence of the Welsh language was another aspect of Wales that made it seem such a foreign country. Although these English travellers found that English was spoken by shop- and innkeepers and the Welsh gentry, Welsh was the lingua franca of the majority of the people, and the diarists were fascinated by the 'foreignness' of it all. Mary Russell is near Cardiff when she gets into conversation with a local woman whom she says:

> . . . spoke English pretty well but with the peculiar tone & emphasis which they all have & which quite resembles that of a foreigner that is learning to speak the English language . . . it seemed to strike me as a very strong unintelligible jargon. On Sunday however we went to hear a Welsh man preach in his native tongue & were very much pleased with the sound of the language; the tones were varied & soft & we supposed he must have been esteemed an eloquent preacher. *(30th July 1804)*

Cardiff castle (Sarah Wilmot, 1802)

Thus, with its wild countryside, strange (to English ears) language, and religious non-conformity, travelling to Wales for pleasure must have seemed almost as foreign as travelling to Europe; and the early diarists, in particular, seemed to feel themselves truly 'abroad', with their diaries reflecting all the excitement that being in a new and strange environment can bring.

Chapter 2

The Inquisitive Travellers:
Frances Anne Crewe (1795) and
Sarah Anne Wilmot (1795 and 1802)

Seariously this mountain beats everything I ever saw since I was a Child in Italy! It is true I have seen Snowdon at a distance, but then that stands in a Range of other Mountains, & it seems that it is its highest point only that beats this, & in all Snowdonia there are no rocks so uniformly high as this Guiguantic one.

Frances Anne Crewe, 22nd August 1795

The peculiar beauties of this river [Wye], attracting so many travellers have taught the people of Ross to provide pleasure boats for their accommodation. They are built to hold ten persons commodiously, have an awning to shelter from rain or sun; a table to draw or regale upon; lockers to hold books, or bottles and benches for four or five men to navigate the boat. In one of these we set sail on the sweetest, mildest morning with every disposition in Life to be pleased.

Sarah Anne Wilmot, 11th August 1795

Two very different women visited Wales in August 1795. The first, Frances Anne Crewe, a noted beauty and socialite, explored the grandeur of the north; whilst the second, Sarah Anne Wilmot, enjoyed the gentler beauties of the south.

Frances (1748–1818) was extremely well-known in her time. She was the only daughter of the poetess Frances Greville and her husband Fulke Greville, 'man of fashion', diplomat and politician, and was reputed to be one of the most beautiful women of her day. On 4th April 1776, when only eighteen, she married John Crewe, who later became the first Baron Crewe. As well as having four children, two of whom died in infancy, Frances led a colourful private life, finding time for politics, the arts and affairs. By the age of 20 she was an ardent supporter of Charles James Fox, the fast-living, womanising, radical Whig politician and, as a Whig hostess, she canvassed actively for him when he was seeking parliamentary election in 1784. Her beauty led to her being painted three times by Sir Joshua Reynolds; she also had an affair with the playwright Richard Brinsley Sheridan, who dedicated his play *The School for Scandal* to her. When the affair ended in 1788 Sheridan complained about her 'self pitying and depressive nature', yet, whatever her personal mood, Frances continued her political activities with unabated energy. By 1793 she

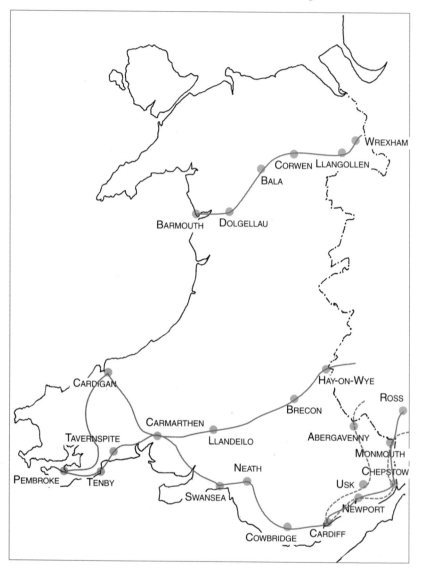

Frances Crewe and Sarah Wilmot.
1795: Frances Crewe travelled from Wrexham to Barmouth and back.
1795: Sarah Wilmot did a circular tour of south Wales.
1802: Sarah Wilmot revisited south Wales, travelling as far as Cardiff
and then leaving Wales via Abergavenny.

was organising a committee of ladies to raise money for French refugee clergy, and in 1796 she supported Edmund Burke in his attempt to start a school for French refugee children. On her death she was said to have been 'one of the most brilliant constellations in the hemisphere of fashion'.

Sarah was the second wife of John Wilmot, member of Parliament and lawyer. Like Frances Crewe, one of his many duties was raising money for French refugee clergy. It is thus likely that the two women would have known each other, although I suspect that the flamboyant Frances might not have been particularly well liked by Sarah. I can imagine them meeting, perhaps on a cold winter's evening, in an elegant drawing room in London, and discovering that they had both done a Welsh Tour earlier that year. Had Sarah shown Frances her diary, with its fine handwriting and even finer watercolours, Frances, whose unillustrated Welsh diary was hastily written in a scrawling untidy hand, might have felt just a little envious of Sarah's finer and more artistic work.

From the tone and content of her diaries, Sarah emerges as a rather serious person – as, it would seem, was her husband, for contemporary accounts describe John Wilmot as 'an upright man of unimpeachable character'. Yet this did not prevent scandal in his personal life. In 1776, when he was twenty-seven, he had married the sixteen year-old Frances Sainthill. After the birth of their fifth child Frances ran off with her groom and John divorced her in 1792.[1] A year later he married Sarah. She seems to have loved her husband dearly for in her diaries she refers to him fondly as her 'Mr W', her 'caro' and her 'dear invalid'. After the traumas of his first wife's infidelity, marriage to the loving Sarah must have proved a blessing.[2]

Sadly, this second marriage also had its share of tragedy, as Ann and Percival, the two children of the marriage, both died in infancy. I have been unable to trace Ann's baptism, and even Percival's raises a question. Records show that on 2nd April 1797 a 'Percival Eardley son of John Wilmot Esq[uir]e & Susanna Jane his wife was baptised in the parish of St Andrew Holborn'.[3] Although the date and the names of father and son fit with what little is known about Percival, it is curious that the wife's name is different – Susanna Jane instead of Sarah. A mystery? A scandal? History does not tell us.

* * *

When Frances Crewe visited Wales she was, perhaps, hoping to enjoy a respite from both her political activities and sexual intrigues. She is a true 'picturesque' tourist visiting Wales, with Pennant as her guidebook, simply to explore its wild beauty. She is in Wales for only a week, but her diary is full of what she sees, what she learns about and whom she meets. She begins her short holiday by travelling through the beautiful **Vale of Llangollen** where the waterfalls 'being shown in great perfection' compensate for the bad weather. From there she goes on to **Bala** (*Y Bala*) via a rough and hilly road. She has an enforced stay there, caused by what must then have been one of the major hazards of travelling, an injured horse, for she says that:

> . . . one of our horses fell down yesterday, & hurt his knee so much that
> the Coachman is fearful of venturing on today, there are no post horses
> here, & if we lose one whole day out of the short time we have for our
> Journey we shall never see **Cader Idris** [*Cadair Idris*] which is my Great
> ambition! After much deliberation & consultation & many wise plans
> adopted by us all & the minute after rejected, we came to a resolution
> of sending for post horses from **Corwen**, & keeping them as long as we
> wanted them while our own should remain here to recover their
> fatigue. (*21st August 1795*)

While she is waiting, Frances amuses herself by finding out about the
traditions of the country from the innkeeper, in particular the pride the Welsh
felt for the exploits of Owain Glyndŵr, the last Welshman to be called the
Prince of Wales. His reign was short-lived for, although he gained control of
most of Wales by 1404 and established an independent Welsh Parliament at
Machynlleth, English armies soon recaptured the major Welsh cities, leaving
him, until his death in 1416, more of a guerrilla leader than a conquering one.

At last the post horses arrive and Frances and her companions have a
'most enchanting drive' through **Glyndyfrdwy Vale** which many travellers,
she tells us, prefer to the Vale of Llangollen, as it is terminated by 'so sublime
an object as Cader Idris for a Background, but Comparisons if they are not
odious, are at least troublesome & I am sure it is better policy to suppose two
objects to be perfect instead of one' – definitely a 'glass half-full' rather than
'half-empty' attitude to life. Frances makes the mistake that many travellers
today still make, as the mountain she sees from this vale is **Aran Benllyn**, not
Cadair Idris and it is not until she arrives at the 'curious' town of **Dolgellau**
that she actually sees Cadair Idris. In the evening, curiosity leads her to:

> . . . stroll up into some part of our mountain & as the evening was fine
> we were out so long as to alarm the Servants for our safety & when we
> returned to our Inn the landlady (who is an English woman) told us
> they were gone different ways in search of us, but it was quite
> impossible to return home while we had a glimpse of remaining light
> . . . unless you were used to such scenes as these you can have no
> conception of what we beheld this evening . . . all was awful &
> tremendous that we view'd, & the very winds blew in sounds quite
> new to me . . . I stood still to contemplate the whole scene around me
> . . . clouds were passing below the spot I stood upon, & mountains
> over them bursting through still higher clouds almost as if they
> themselves had motion! Heaven & Earth appeared to be entangled, &
> each contending for effect. They lost to my poor eyes all distinctness of
> character 'each seemed either' till the setting sun at last shone forth
> again & relieved me from this strange surprise. (*22nd August 1795*)

This one sortie into the foothills of Cadair Idris is clearly sufficient. Frances
returns to the safety of her inn where she continues to pen many pages about

the wildness of the countryside, the ancient inns where they stop to change horses, the harpers, and the language. She is very conscious of being in a land that is not just wild but also very 'foreign'. She meets 'drovers of Cattle & when we desired the Postilion to ask wither they were going, the Answer was to England. This was one of many small occurrences which reminded me today of being in a foreign country'.

Frances often wanders from her own narrative to quote great chunks from Pennant, but she soon resumes her 'pribbles & prabbles about Wales'. The inn she is staying in, for example, reminds her of German inns she has been in. The rooms, long and with bare walls, are such that 'some persons I know would not like to reside, but we are well paid by what we have already seen, for a few small Inconveniences & after all fatigue is often as good a sauce for sleep'. Whilst staying there she thinks she discovers, probably quite incorrectly, the real origin of the word 'nanny goat', for she is told that it comes from the name of **Nannau**, a mansion near Dolgellau once owned by a family called Nanney, so that 'goats which were called Nanny Goats first came from hence, & this conjecture rather amuses me, because I till now always thought People said Nanny Goats as they say Baa lambs or Moo cows to please Children in a namby pamby way'.

She also comments that since the new Irish road was made, 'a few English persons were even known to stray so far as this!' As Thomas Telford's famous road across north Wales was not started until 1819, Frances was probably referring to the improvements made by John Sylvester in 1772. Before such improvements began, coach journeys in Wales would have been a slow and arduous business, with average speeds, depending on the type of vehicle and the quality or otherwise of the road, being about five miles an hour. She returns to this theme later in her diary when she recalls that, until this new road, 'no mortal liked to venture by the Llangollen roads'.

The next day she travels on to **Barmouth** (*Abermo*) which she, like many other travellers, compares to Gibraltar. She is particularly struck by the great trade of 'woollen Manufactory, you see no women nor Children who are not knitting, & it seems the men knit very much too, but I cannot say I saw more than one man employing himself so'. She later 'buys a pair of men's stockings . . . to keep as a curiosity'. Being a Sunday she decides to attend the Welsh service which she finds 'curious . . . there is a sort of Gutral uncouthness in it to English Ears, but there is also something grand & imposing in some words'. She stays in the busiest of the three inns or, as she says rather tartly, 'public house. We heard that dinner would be served in the hall at 3 o'clock, whether we ordered any or not and we might eat good fish & mutton etc. to a tune on the Harp if we chose it'. She makes some equally acerbic remarks about the people she meets at dinner, which include:

> . . . some very convivial as well as odd persons of both sexes, & among the odd was the famous poetess of Lichfield Miss Seyward who I have no inclination to meet again, tho' for once she was rather entertaining.

She appears to be no longer young, but as if she had been rather handsome tho' upon too large a scale. Her manners & conversation are just what one sees in professed blue stocking Ladies, affected helplessness, & unaffected pedantry, for her discourse always boasted of the Books she had read, & nothing Genuine, nothing engaging in what she said, her Enthusiasm seemed artificial when she describes the impressions which were made upon her mind by the scenery around her . . . I could still have condoled with her in this reasonable affliction [getting her information wrong] if she had not provoked my spleen by abrasively asking me almost as soon as we began our meal & in the presence of the whole table if I was not the Lady celebrated in the famous poem of Mr Fox. What could I say? I was distressed but forced to stammer out the truth which was "yes" & that I considered it a very high honour. She was not satisfied with this for she hallooed out across the table to a Gentleman who was opposite "this Sir is the lady to whom Mr Fox's beautiful poem was addressed". *(23rd August 1795)*

The Miss Seyward mentioned here was probably Anna Seward, the Romantic poetess, known as 'The Swan of Lichfield' in her day; whilst the reference to 'Mr Fox's beautiful poem' refers to a book of poems that Fox had dedicated to Frances some twenty years earlier. Having recovered her composure, Frances is interested to learn about the practice of the Penillion, the art of vocal improvisation over a given melody, with the singer singing a counter-melody over a harp melody, in which:

. . . everybody in the company has to sing a verse round the harp in the most common tune & the easiest (they say) to adapt words to, which they have either invented at the moment, or recollect out of other songs, & no changes or innovation which they ever had in this country have interfered with this very ancient custom. They enjoy it still very much & many very unlearned people are quick at it, & they make matches of Penillions against their Neighbours, sometimes parish against parish . . . I understand that all this poetry & singing is generally accompanied with dancing here, & that on a Sunday evening, even about **Wrexham** (*Wrecsam*), they danced very much of late, but since so many are become Methodists this wholesome innocent amusement has been much left off on Sundays. *(23rd August 1795)*

Barmouth is the furthest extent of her brief sojourn into north Wales and from there Frances starts on her journey homewards, stopping at Llangollen to dine at **Plas Newydd** with the famed 'hermit' ladies (the Ladies of Llangollen). Eleanor Butler and Sarah Ponsonby had, some years earlier, eloped from Ireland to set up a new life together in Wales where their Gothic residence became a magnet for writers and intellectuals. They were very much part of the tourist experience of the period, with the more honoured tourists being invited into their home, as was Frances, whilst the less honoured simply peeked at them as they strolled about their property. Frances describes how the 'hermits':

> . . . live so secluded from the world . . . & never stir for any time together from this Romantic place. They are obliging & polite to all travellers who come recommended . . . we walked over the whole of this little Paradise . . . these Ladies lived at a distance from all society for a long time after they sheltered themselves in this wild spot, & they were first discovered by their Neighbours to be of the Better sort, by some Charitable acts they performed in their scattered Hamlet . . . their discourse is Cheerful, Obligeing, & Indulgent, there is no vain Cant, or stupid pride about themselves in anything they say. *(24th August 1795)*

After this fine hospitality, Frances has a rude awakening when she reaches the inn at Wrexham, for she would have liked to have had:

> . . . better lodges, as the day was warm & the noise of the town by so much military going through it did not bring to mind the purling streams & gurgling brooks nor dashing waterfalls we had been so familiar with of late, but the landlady told us that Mr Wilkinson (the iron factor) had a right to the best apartment whenever he came into the Town, & as some modern Philosophers rather wish to destroy all old fashioned gallantry from their own sex to ours, I was not surprised he enjoyed himself . . . all the evening in the Grand apartment & triumphed over us, poor ladies in our little parlour next to the street below. "Oh Madam (says the landlady) Mr Wilkinson made a bargain he should always have the best apartment & once when the house was full & Sir Watkin was living upstairs with the militia, he had him turned out because of his right". *(25th August 1795)*

The two characters mentioned here are the ironmaster John Wilkinson and Sir Watkin Williams Wynn, fifth baronet. John Wilkinson was the founder of the New Bersham Company of ironworks that led the world in the field of iron technology at that time; whilst Sir Watkin was a rich and powerful landowner, with a house at nearby Wynnstay. It is interesting that the manufacturer, who would have been 'new money', is able to oust the landed gentry, who would have been 'old money', from the best apartment.

As Frances travels back towards England she muses about her trip, writing that she would like to revisit some of these beautiful places, as she 'likes to look at some places twice & to enjoy them with repose sometimes, rather than to be always stunned by amazement & admiration as I have been lately!' She feels that she has really only scratched the surface of this magnificent country, rather ruefully describing herself as one of those 'Clodpole travellers . . . who have . . . nothing but General Enthusiasm, without patriotism to inspire. To us, very much is lost!'

Once back at **Crewe Hall** in Cheshire, her grand and comfortable home

Frances looks over her 'little Welch Journal' in order to add anything remembered after the event. She comments on the coach stages and the state of the roads, the towns and the good provisions. The inns she found to be dirty, although she was often told that they were soon to be improved. As for the people, they look 'comfortable & happy [and] are much more cheerful & cordial in their manners than the English people . . . I don't recollect meeting any beggars except a very few little tumbling children on the road'. Frances is sensitive to the fact that English history books do not do justice to Welsh history, and suggests that the reading of Welsh historians and antiquarians might help English people have a deeper understanding of the richness of Welsh history and heritage.

And so her diary ends, with Frances encouraging her readers to:

> . . . pray, make this Journey yourself; remember I do not recommend these Countries as Constant Habitations for I believe many Inconveniences would be Experienced, which we all Escape who live Elsewhere, but Excursions Like these are pleasant Episodes in ordinary life, & afford wholesome, as well as Cheerfull Holidays to the Imagination! Finis. *(30th August 1795)*

* * *

Sarah Wilmot's two visits to south Wales were very different from Frances Crewe's dash round north Wales. On both occasions she and John take a

Raglan castle (Sarah Wilmot, 1802)

leisurely twelve-week tour through southern England and Wales, spending about five weeks in Wales on their first visit and three weeks on their second.

Research into Sarah's diaries provided one of those serendipitous discoveries that make history such fun. Early in my researches I had seen Sarah Wilmot's 1802 diary in the library of the National Museum of Wales in Cardiff. Sometime later I found, in the Wigan archives, a small leather-bound, illustrated journal by a Sarah *Haslam*. As I read it I had a real sense of déjà vu, as much of it echoed the Cardiff journal. The subsequent discovery that Haslam was Sarah's maiden name made it clear that the journal in the Wigan archives was the one that Sarah would have written on her travels, together with the sketches she did on the spot; the Cardiff journal was clearly written up later, possibly on long winter evenings, when some of the 'rough' sketches were worked up into more polished water-colours, presumably so that it could be read and admired by her family and friends. What made this find so interesting was that the 'rough' Wigan diary had sketches that were, in some respects, livelier than those in the more polished version, as well as sketches that she omitted altogether in her later copy. It was also a much fuller account of her travels, with more 'human' content in terms of her comments on people as well as places.

Sarah, who describes herself as a 'female antiquary', is also travelling in search of the picturesque, and so she and John begin their trip to Wales with the Wye tour. These trips actually began in 1745, but gained in popularity after the Revd. Gilpin published his *Observations*, with poets and painters including Coleridge, Wordsworth and Turner all visiting the Wye valley, and with 'ordinary' tourists following in their footsteps to see the various 'picturesque' viewpoints listed by Gilpin. Sarah and John set sail on their river tour on 11th August 1795 from **Ross-on-Wye** and Sarah's comments, as she glides down the Wye in the boat, give glimpses of a lost world. On one bank there is a large iron foundry where 'black and curling clouds of smoke issued from the noisy furnace; on the other bank rich, verdant pasture with clumps of stately Oak & Beech'. At **Coldwell** a little party of 'cottagers' conducts them to a summit of 'jutting rocks, verdant turf and waving trees'. From the summit they see not only the meandering Wye, but also the places where 'lime kilns [are] smoking among the cottages, the iron mills clanging in direful din, the river hurrying in a rapid fall to quit the terrors of the noisy scene'.

Sarah enquires of the cottagers how they live and finds that 'bread was too scarce & too dear for them to buy . . . & of other meat they never bought any, they liv'd on potatoes & vegetables'. She expresses concern that if too much corn is exported down the river 'in this time of general scarcity, it is an evil to be justly complained of, our greatest blessings may be perverted & become our heaviest grievances'. She later observes the custom of the poor of cutting 'ferns . . . which they burn to ashes, then wet & mix into paste, then work it in to balls which they sell for washing & whitening blankets & flannel, in spinning & weaving, of which the industrious poor find their principal employment & support'.

Sarah and John spend their first night in Wales at the **Beaufort Arms** in **Monmouth** (*Trefynwy*). Sarah damns both the inn and Monmouth with faint praise, 'tolerably' being her favourite word. Monmouth is a 'tolerably good town' although the Castle is 'metamorphosed into a pigsty'; the inn is 'very dirty, but tolerably good fare'. Throughout her trip Sarah can be a waspish as well as an enthusiastic diarist. **Raglan Castle** (*Castell Raglan*), although 'a fine Gothic ruin . . . is indifferent as to picturesque beauty, water being wanted to complete the scene'. **Tredegar House**, now seen as one of the most outstanding Restoration houses in the whole of Britain, is described by Sarah as being 'in the old dreary style'; whilst **Piercefield**, although the new mansion had yet to be finished, does not seem to be 'strikingly elegant'. However the formal parkland with its cliff-top walk does excite her interest. This walk, which had been created by an earlier owner Valentine Morris, a wealthy West Indies planter, ran along the Wye valley high above the river; trees had been felled to provide views and there were various points of interest, such as a grotto, temple, and bath house. Although some tourists admired the house rather more than Sarah seems to have done, it was these walks that made Piercefield such a magnet for the early tourists. Indeed Sarah finds that 'nature has done so much as to leave little for Art to improve'.

On their second day on the river Sarah and John sail on to the great Cistercian abbey of **Tintern** (*Tyndyrn*), 'memorable for a faux pas in the female antiquary mistaking an old barn for the expected abbey, & beginning to make a sketch!' Once she had discovered her mistake, not a word of criticism finds its way into Sarah's diary, for she sees before her an abbey:

> . . . embosom'd in screens of stately trees, on all sides various & on all sides lovely!! itself most lovely!! Seated on a soft green velvet carpet, surrounded by the gentle Wye . . . the columns & arches are clothed with the finest ivy which hangs & clings with great luxuriance in graceful drapery or gay festoons & forms a verdant canopy to guard the walls. The roof is entirely gone, but the fine blue sky afforded us a cheering light . . . & the sunbeams at intervals increased the native beauties which surrounded us! (*12th August 1795*)

Sarah eventually tears herself away from these delights and the boat sails on to **Chepstow** (*Cas-gwent*), 'with the scenery continuing to be very grand: large Amphitheatres of perpendicular Rocks . . . the river wide the reaches long with screens of hanging wood of finest growth & foliage'. Despite her comments on what she does not find to her taste, Sarah's happiness bubbles over time and time again in her diary and the Wye tour seems to have been her little piece of paradise for to 'have seen as we have with such weather, with such a Party! & with such a kind Pilot, guide & Friend, is an advantage & a happiness that few can boast of!!!'

Sarah finds Chepstow a prettier town than Monmouth, with houses that are 'white with parapets & mostly sash'd, the inhabitants look neat &

'They ran large homes and enjoyed genteel activities': Frederica Rouse Boughton, 1861.

'The dress of the women consists of a striped flannel petticoat & a long brown jacket over it, a blue handkerchief tyed over their heads & a black beaver hat upon that': Sarah Wilmot, 1795.
(Drawing of Welsh Fashions Taken on a Market-Day in Wales, 1851)

Orielton, where, in 1808, Millicent Bant thought there were 'as many windows as days in the year'.

Plas Newydd today, former home of the Ladies of Llangollen. In 1795 Frances Crewe 'walked over the whole of this little Paradise'.

The orangery at Margam today. In 1824 Margaret Martineau wrote that 'the late Mr Talbot built the orangery ... and preserved the ruins from further decay and then found that he had come to the end of his purse and soon after his life'.

Newport was 'a very good [town] & the people very civil', Millicent Bant found in 1808.

In 1823, Mary Anne Hibbert commented that Monmouth was a 'handsome well-built town, but it is not at all picturesque'.

The drive to Dolgellau was 'beautiful beyond description ... there is but one Inn, which is surrounded with Pig Sties, nothing to be got but fried Mutton Chops': Millicent Bant, 1806.

Parys Mountain as it is today. In 1806 Millicent Bant found it 'a most curious, interesting, awful & infernal place'.

A genteel ride in Pugh's cart:
Frederica Rouse Boughton, 1860.

Conwy Castle as it is today. In 1824 Margaret Martineau found that it
'was fine but it is such a hackneyed subject that it did not strike
one as new'.

Pont Aberglaslyn, which Mary Anne Hibbert saw during 'a very beautiful walk' in 1849.

Tredegar House today. It was 'a fine old place' even when Millicent Bant saw it in 1808.

A portrait of Frederica (in red) as a child.

After the holiday – Frederica back home in Downton:
Frederica Rouse Boughton, 1860.

'There are only a few fragments left now of very old masonry all in detached bits': Frederica Rouse Boughton in 1860, on climbing Dinas Brân.

'We came to a high stone wall right across the path, over which a queer little ladder had been contrived': Frederica Rouse Boughton on the Precipice Walk in 1860.

'The fall burst suddenly upon us & it was beautiful ... it comes dashing gloriously down from the heights':
Frederica Rouse Boughton, on Pistyll Mawddach in 1860.

'Oh such a pretty little cave ... almost buried in the luxuriant fern & heather that grew round the entrance': Frederica Rouse Boughton, 1860.

Another genteel ride in Pugh's cart: Frederica Rouse Boughton, 1860.

Visiting Nannau in Pugh's cart: Frederica Rouse Boughton, 1860.

43

'An amusing encounter with a troop of small boys':
Frederica Rouse Boughton, 1860.

'Three small children ... with a big black bottle':
Frederica Rouse Boughton, 1860.

On the Barmouth road: Frederica Rouse Boughton, 1860.

'They all pressed round us, teasing and bothering for half pennies':
Frederica Rouse Boughton, 1860.

The ponies 'were all varieties of colour ... they were such a rough untidy picturesque lot': Frederica Rouse Boughton, 1860.

'A group of girls, all tumbled down in picturesque attitudes in a huge bundle of dried ferns': Frederica Rouse Boughton, 1860.

'The fog was ever so thick':
Frederica Rouse Boughton on her ascent of Cadair Idris, 1860.

'The cloud rolled away for a few minutes ... it was lovely':
Frederica Rouse Boughton on Cadair Idris, 1860.

The farmhouse was 'a rather gloomy looking place':
Frederica Rouse Boughton, 1860.

'The quaint aspect of the old kitchen ... and the delightful woman
standing over the boiling pot':
Frederica Rouse Boughton, 1860.

comfortable, here is a dock for ships . . . the Castle is situated on a perpendicular rock overhanging the river Wye, an interesting and picturesque ruin'. Leaving Chepstow, Sarah pursues her journey 'with renovated spirits & delight thro' a sweet, cultivated country; in some places haymaking in one meadow, & wheat reaping in the next'. Before long, however, this piece of rural paradise is shattered by the 'mean, dirty town' of Newport, where the Castle 'has lately been repair'd for a jail'.

The next town on her travels is Cardiff, which impresses her a good deal. The **Cardiff Arms** promises cleanliness and comfort, houses are 'white plaister or stucco with slated roofs, the streets are airy, paved & clean'. The castle is 'interesting rather than grand or picturesque', whilst **Caerphilly Castle** *(Castell Caerffili)* is full of:

> . . . gloomy & gigantic terrors . . . massive circular towers, dangerous galleries, dismal dungeons, vaults & battlements, all calculated for resisting force but now evidently yielding with reluctance to the destructive hand of time . . . [and which] excite the wonder rather than the admiration of the female antiquary. *(15th August 1795)*

As she travels further into south Wales, Sarah's comments become briefer, perhaps not surprisingly, for she travels nearly every day, usually for thirty or more miles, so that much of the day would be spent in the coach or waiting for the horses to be changed. Nevertheless she still makes some interesting observations. She finds **Cowbridge** *(Bont-faen)*, where she stays in the 'middling' **Bear Inn**, a pretty town with neat cottages, 'many of them with 6 rooms & a good garden & orchard . . . provisions are very cheap'. Cowbridge is still a pretty town but is now more likely to sell expensive gourmet provisions and smart clothes. As she travels on through the rural **Vale of Glamorgan**, Sarah continues to note the cost of provisions, as well as the fact that the 'mangel-wurzel which answers very well for cattle' is cultivated.

On her journey west, Sarah's next stop is at **Margam** where, once again, her expectations are 'sorely dashed'. Although Margam, like Tintern, was once a Cistercian monastery, the estate passed into the hands of the Mansel family after the Dissolution and the abbey fell into disrepair, although a 'faire and sumptious house' was built on the site. This was demolished between 1786 and 1793 by the then owner, Thomas Mansel Talbot, who built a mighty orangery in the garden, longer and more capacious than any other in Britain. Yet for Sarah this is a mere 'greenhouse', whilst the rest is 'a jumble of modern antiques: Temples, church & Chapter house unfortunately crowded into a Cow-yard . . . although the 'orange, lemon, citron [larger and less acid than the lemon] & shaddocks [citrus fruit resembling an orange but much larger] . . . were numerous & healthy, but not near as large as I have seen at Kew'.

After this disappointment Sarah stops next in industrial **Neath** *(Castell-nedd)*, where she visits the wealthy industrialist Sir Herbert Mackworth at his fine house, **The Gnoll**. Sarah ignores both house and parkland, for it is

Mackworth's copper works that fascinate her – although her reaction to these is ambivalent in the extreme. On the one hand she views 'these direful Machinations with terror & disgust'. On the other, viewed in a commercial light, 'they are curious & interesting . . . I lament these matters do not properly belong to female enquiry, as I should like to understand these links in the great Chain of Commerce'. From here, Sarah dashes on to Swansea, where she stays in the 'dirty, bad' **Mackworth Arms** and finds that:

> . . . a good society is kept up among the inhabitants who are chiefly English, settled there on plans of economy, they have a weekly Ball & excellent musick . . . the bathing is not good, being too distant from the town for invalids, the Cottagers & Mechanics appear dirty, indeed filthy in their persons & houses, the women very ragged and slatternly in their apparel, generally without shoes & stockings & apparently employed in the meanest & most laborious drudgery . . . a sort of native courtesy prevails among this poor class. *(18th August 1795)*

Leaving the copper works and dirt behind her Sarah rides through a rich country to **Carmarthen** (*Caerfyrddin*), 'a clean town'. En route, unlike many of the travellers, she gets off the beaten track and visits **Laugharne** (*Lacharn*), a 'remarkably pleasant village . . . one of the most beautiful we have yet seen in Wales . . . castle still a most grand & picturesque ruin . . . handsome church shaded by a number of tall & graceful Ash-trees, the houses neat, comfortable & mostly thatch'd'. She and John also have a memorable meal there with 'fish . . . 2 fowls, roast veal, Bacon, salad, greens & potatoes, tarts, cheese, butter, Ale, Beer & a bottle of good Port, the charge was for dinner 5sh. Wine 2.6d. Beer 1sh. in total 8/6d'.

From Carmarthen, Sarah's route takes her to **Tenby** (*Dinbych-y-pysgod*) through countryside of 'varied beauty of cultivation & fertility . . . where many fields of waving corn promised a golden harvest to their Owners!' Lovely though the countryside was, some of the inns still left much to be desired, with the **Princes Feathers** at **Tavernspite** being 'the dirtiest & most filthy we had rested in'. Sarah stops at Tenby six days, where, unless she had servants with her, it must have been a relief to have a break from the constant packing and unpacking of clothes. Her comments on the **White Lion** provide a clue that she might well have been travelling with servants, even though they are not mentioned at all in her diary, for their accommodation is far more than would be needed by just two people. It consists of 'a handsome sitting room opposite the sea, 4 excellent sleeping rooms for which charged nothing . . . we never sat down to fewer than eleven dishes'.

She gets off the beaten track again when she visits **Caldey Island** (*Ynys Bŷr*), at that time a treeless island abounding in rabbits. Today Caldey is home to a community of Cistercian monks, and there are now several acres of woodland, with the farmland being grazed by a prime beef herd rather than rabbits. As the sea journey was choppy and unsettling to the stomach,

Sarah may well have wondered if the trip was worth her while, but far more unsettling than a choppy sea are the customs she finds in Tenby, which do much to upset her sense of propriety. First there is the bathing which:

> . . . might be made perfectly commodious without any other expense than common sense, but whether that ingredient which everyone thinks he possesses be exchanged on the road for the current coin of taking things as they are found, the Ladies & Gents go in close together, opposite the most publick street, in the broad face of the sun, & of every idle observer, to the disgrace of common decency! *(28th August 1795)*

Sarah's comment on 'taking things as they are found' is probably her modest way of saying that a good deal of nudity could be seen. At that time, women bathers would descend into the sea from a bathing machine and then splash about naked beneath the canopy; whilst men were naked when they swam. Sarah was not the only one to be outraged, for by-laws were later passed to deal with this 'immodest' behaviour. As well as the nudity, there was dancing but the 'weekly ball for cards & dancing is held . . . not on the best plan, the hours are too late, the music very bad & no Master of Ceremonies . . . the continued influx of the English has raised prices of some articles to a degree of which the frugal Inhabitants justly complain'.

After what must have nevertheless been a relaxing few days Sarah rides on to **Pembroke** *(Penfro)* travelling through 'wide rich valleys adorn'd with handsome churches, & scattered villages, bounded with the distant mountains . . . & a fine open sea enriched with numerous vessels'. She takes

Bathing place in Cardigan Bay near Aberystwyth, by J Hassell, 1790s.

a detour to visit **Carew Castle**, 'a fine ruin' and examines a 'stone column . . . with characters deeply engraved on 2 sides, but we cou'd gain no intelligence of its use or intention'. This is in fact an eleventh-century Celtic cross. From Pembroke, where she stays for three days, Sarah visits **Stackpole Court**:

> . . . a good house, badly situated; the whole estate undergoing great alteration . . . the kitchen & flower gardens . . . the conservatories, hot house & green house in great style! but bad taste . . . the plantations are greatly injured by the sea breezes & various defects in the soil with injudicious planting have robb'd the trees of their principal beauties viz. grace, strength & foliage'. *(30th August 1795)*

She also takes a boat trip to **Haverfordwest** (*Hwlffordd*) which was a busy port, trading 'pottery & various Articles . . . for flannel, paper, Lime, and Corn'. From Pembroke Sarah turns north-east towards **Cardigan** (*Aberteifi*), travelling through a barren countryside in which the villagers 'must endure many, many hard months in every year of their suffering existence, wild cranberries are the only produce of this extensive heath, the people dig the turf for fuel . . . not a single tree offers shade to man or beast'. At Cardigan, where the **Black Lion** offers 'clean & good accommodation', Sarah finds the town:

> . . . small & poor, the houses very humble habitations tho' said to be inhabited by wealthy & genteel people, the gaol is building . . . here is no manufactory & very little employment for the poor . . . the streets are fill'd with dirty, ragged & idle children. The dress of the women . . . consists of a striped flannel petticoat & a long brown jacket over it, a blue handkerchief tyed over their heads & a black beaver hat upon that, a large brown, or blue flannel wrapper which goes round the waist & over the shoulders & serves the double purpose of a cloak & cradle for the one or two children they generally carry at their back. *(2nd September 1795)*

From here Sarah takes what is clearly a most enjoyable river trip to **Cilgerran Castle**, the legendary site from which, in 1109, Princess Nest, wife of the Earl of Pembroke, and Wales's answer to Helen of Troy, was abducted by Owain, a prince of Powys. Sarah was either oblivious to this scandal or forbore to mention it in her diary, simply commenting on the next site, Sir Benjamin Hammet's tin works:

> . . . at present in their infancy, but gigantic & terrible enough for their age, they employ 200 labourers & appear to be plann'd on a very extensive scale, but the Proprietor is very doubtful whether they will answer the expense he has been at, as he neither understands the nature or progress of the works himself, it is very probable that they will never repay him. *(3rd September 1795)*

Sarah was correct in this assumption, for Benjamin Hammet died a few years later without the works ever being profitable for him, and in 1806 his son closed them down. The next day Sarah takes a ride to the famous salmon leap at **Cenarth**, and then has dinner with Sir Benjamin Hammet in his house, **Castell Malgwyn**. After this second break from travelling Sarah starts her homeward journey, retracing her steps to Carmarthen via **Newcastle Emlyn** (*Castell Newydd Emlyn*), 'a shabby little town' where, although only eleven o'clock but 'being very hungry we regaled ourselves with eggs & bacon'. From here the journey provides considerable excitement for the hilly road seems like a 'journey to the skies, beginning with a mountain 4 miles high by slow but (thank GOD) sure degrees' to the summit. The horses at least were rewarded for their hard work, as they are rested and fed at the summit, before carrying Sarah and John into Carmarthen and to a warm welcome at the **New Ivy Bush** coaching inn.

As the next day is a Sunday, Sarah and John go to church before setting off again to find that at **Llandeilo** even the 'dullest traveller must be awaken'd to a sense of pleasure in viewing such a Paradise . . . it is one of those masterpieces in nature which must be seen to be sufficiently admired'. Sarah duly admires all that she sees – the limpid river, the richly adorned valley, the native Welsh castle of **Dryslwyn** which is the summit of perfection – all in all, she muses, Merlin's magic must still prevail here, so perhaps it is the intrusion of the 'real' world into this paradise that makes Sarah surprisingly unsympathetic about the poverty she sees, for:

> . . . the excessive sloth of the common people amounts almost to a nuisance, their dwellings are so offensive as to incommode foot passengers & their appearance so very dirty as to make them objects of disgust. Poverty does not seem to be their excuse, as their clothes are not so ragged, as they are filthy in themselves, & it wou'd be of general utility to the country if parish officers cou'd be appointed to keep infection from their houses . . . another sign of barbarism . . . namely, they have divided the churchyard & made a road to pass from one part of the Town to another . . . [and] the sacred mansions of their departed Ancestors are hourly disturb'd by business . . . & hogs & horses fatten on their graves! The Rector of the Parish wou'd do well to correct this abuse! (*7th September 1795*)

Such high dudgeon is, however, short-lived and followed in the next diary breath with a 'most delightful ride to see the ruins of **Carreg Cennan Castle**'. One of the most dramatically situated castles in Wales, it was, and still is, impossible to reach other than on foot, but Sarah with her 'spirit of curiosity & perseverance with walking, climbing & scrambling' reaches the summit.

Two days later Sarah, now well on her homeward journey, arrives at Brecon. Despite it being the 'handsomest' town she has visited and 'lovely beyond comparison', Sarah still finds all her senses being assaulted by the 'dirt & the smells from hogs, dogs & various causes.' She nevertheless spends several days there, 'viewing & reviewing these delightful scenes', before turning the horses towards England. On leaving Wales she writes, as did Frances Crewe before her, a summing up of her impressions. Despite her occasional tirades she has clearly enjoyed her holiday enormously, and ends her diary on this happy note:

> . . . there is something pleasant in observing the local manners, habits & customs of a Country remote from the Metropolis. Wales indeed still claims the privilege of independence, & title of ancient & unconquered Britons . . . they preserve their Language & their pedigree uncontaminated, they resist as much as possible any foreign settlers in their country . . . Nature & art have combined to make S. Wales appear so uniformly picturesque . . . [with] Oak, hazel, Birch, black & white thorn, woodbine & wild roses. (*16th September 1795*)

Seven years later Sarah and John return to south Wales for a similar but much shorter tour. Unlike the 1795 journey, when Sarah set off in high spirits, on this August day in 1802 she is feeling sad and gloomy. Although she travels with 'a family party' she does not seem to have any very young children with her and it may well be that, by this time, both her children had died, for she says:

> . . . there is nothing better calculated to dispel the gloom of care, the anxiety of Family, & the disappointments of Life than through the serenity of the Country, the various beauties of Nature & the contented faces you generally see in every industrious Individual you meet on the road; with this hope & expectation we set off . . . under unexpected agitation from the Common Course of casual disappointments & reached the White Horse at Uxbridge . . . here the Power of Nature began her soothing operations and in proportion as the atmosphere cleared & rarified & wafted on "her winnowing wings" the healing breeze of harmony & peace our enjoyments encreased, & social love & social converse past away both time & space. (*20th August 1802*)

As in 1795 Sarah takes the Wye tour from Ross, putting into practice Frances Crewe's wish to revisit places in order to enjoy them in repose. However, on this second trip her agitated mood seems echoed by the weather and instead of the perfect weather of her 1795 tour, there is rain and more rain, although it stops long enough to enable Sarah to climb up to **Symonds Yat**, where she is surrounded by 'all the charms that Nature can bestow Wood, Rock, Mountains, Plains & Water!' Sarah is most affected by the poverty of her guide:

> . . . a young woman with a lovely infant in her arms & a boy of four years and seven months old were our guides; they were cloth'd in rags but clean & in the mother's face patient resignation sat personified.

She had been married six years and seven months & had 3 children living – her husband earn'd 6 shillings a week which was all they could earn, as she had always had Infants to nurse & they pd. 5s a yr. to Ld. Gage for rent. Luxuries are purchased too dearly when misery like this pays. (*24th August 1802*)

Next day she and John are taken by Charles Heath to the **Kymin**, a hill above Monmouth, to see not only the extensive view, but also the small circular banqueting hall used by the local gentry for lunch parties, and the recently erected naval temple. Less than a week before, Charles Heath, a noted local historian, antiquarian and publisher, who much enjoyed taking tourists around his area, had escorted Lord Nelson and Sir William and Emma Hamilton on the same tour. This perhaps explains why Sarah's lively pencil sketch of him in her Wigan journal shows him strutting proudly forward with his hat in his hand, umbrella under his arm, his long, beaky nose looking positively luminescent. Sarah's sad mood gradually begins to lift as the beauty she has come to see diverts her, for she feels she is seeing 'all the wonders of the World – the scenery is rich beyond description, & by the attention of Mr. Heath we had the advantage of seeing the curiosities of the Country much better than by ourselves'. After visiting the Kymin the party goes to the **Buckstone**:

. . . an immense Rock 38 yards in circumference at top about 30 feet high standing on its own irregular base of 9 feet to the earth – its appearance is so tremendous that a number of the people at

The Buckstone (Sarah Wilmot, 1802)

Monmouth assembled with 16 horses & strong Iron chains which they
fasten'd to the slender base & then by every means urged the horses so
attached to throuw it down, but all in vain . . . it is said it has the
property of a rocking stone & can be moved with hand but that is not
true! *(25th August 1802)*

Sarah was wrong about this as it was a logan stone, that is, a stone which was
so finely balanced that it could be rocked to and fro simply by pushing it
gently. In 1885, however, it was tipped from its plinth, allegedly by a group
of travelling actors from London, but such was the public outcry that it was
replaced. Alas, it no longer rocks and today is so surrounded by trees that it
has nothing like the same dramatic appeal. For Sarah it 'displays one of those
unanswerable proofs of the Power of the Divine Architect which no human
Being can Comprehend or dare to imitate'. In the secular world of the
twenty-first century this natural and unaffected way of writing about
religious belief can seem unusual, but such gratitude to the 'Divine Architect'
is common amongst the diarists.

Sarah and John now continue their river trip but it rains heavily again
and, although at Tintern Sarah bravely 'makes a few slight sketches', she is
glad to take shelter at the **Anchor Inn**, 'where the good woman boil'd us
some potatoes, made us a good fire & we dry'd our shoes etc. & having eaten
our Cold Collation the sun gave us a Cheer'. She sails on to Chepstow, where
she arrives, after her wetting in Tintern, with clothes and shoes damp but
with spirits high. She stays at the '**Beaufort Arms**, fine hotel & dear souls . .
. visited Persfield [Piercefield] just purchased by Mr. Wells a Creole'.
Nathaniel Wells was indeed black – the son of a plantation owner on St Kitts
and one of his slaves. He had been given his freedom by his Welsh father,
educated in London, and then had most of his father's considerable estate
left to him. He purchased Piercefield in July 1802 and in 1818 became the first
black High Sheriff in Britain.

Leaving Chepstow on August 29th Sarah goes on to Newport, about
which she is more complimentary than on her previous visit, then on beyond
Cardiff to the Vale of Glamorgan. She takes a look into the churchyard at
Llantwit Major (*Llanilltud Fawr*), where she sees 'several very curious
monumental stones with old Latin or Welsh descriptions which serve to
puzzle the Antiquarians'. These, like the cross at Carew that had also puzzled
her on her earlier visit, are ancient Celtic crosses. Sarah now goes from the
religious to the secular by visiting **St Donat's Castle**, perched on a cliff above
the coast near Cowbridge. She is very impressed by this 'stately' castle which
is 'evidently form'd for splendour and defence. In the banqueting room . . .
the chimney piece, wainscot & ceiling are of carved oak . . . over the former
a collosal bust of Cleopatra in very rude stone sculpture'. There are also
many apartments let to those who seek sea air and sea bathing and are
'willing to purchase health in exchange for the luxuries or even the
certainties of life, as no food can be purchas'd here'.

Two events occur here that Sarah feels are worthy of noting in her diary.

First, she and her party of gentlemen and ladies experience 'another instance of the kindness and unsuspicious simplicity of this worthy people . . . we sat under an oak to wait for our carriage . . . a maid servant bro't us on a neat waiter a loaf, a large piece of cheese, a bottle of wine & some fresh water'. They are then asked if they would take the niece of their benefactress to Cowbridge in their coach. This they agree to do, and the niece:

> . . . a fine rosy young woman of 17 yrs. stepped into the Coach without further ceremony. She din'd with us & in the evening walk'd home to her father, who was either the doctor or Curate of Cowbridge! Where is the Mother, Aunt or Cousin who cou'd have dared to trust a girl of that age to any party on the road; tho' deck'd with coronets . . . hail happy land! where all the women are virtuous! & all the men pure in heart! *(1st September 1802)*

At this point on her second journey Sarah starts wending her way home, stopping at **Caerleon**, the famous Roman town that affords:

> . . . much entertainment to the lovers of Antiquity, the inhabitants collect a tolerable addition to their subsistence by pointing out the remains of Roman Splendour or the more pleasing magnificence of Arthur's hospitality – hence a field is shewn in which is traced a hollow space of 70 yds. called Arthur's round Table or a Roman Theatre – many remains of Roman wells, a famous Tile with Roman Letters inscrib'd L C G 2d Augustus – several Coins & various other curious & interesting circumstances give great celebrity to the Town. *(2nd September 1802)*

When she passes **Llangybi Castle** she has one of her tirades, both against profligate landlords, and architecture which does not conform to her idea of the picturesque. Sarah finds that the castle 'from ill management or neglect loses more than half its beauty & as a residence all its comfort', whilst 'the ruin is considerable but not picturesque'. Llangybi actually had two castles and a house. Remains of a medieval castle can still be seen in woodland, while the earlier Norman castle has, other than its motte, all but disappeared. The 'castle' that Sarah refers to, a late seventeenth-century house, no longer survives.

At **Usk** *(Brynbuga)* her spirits are soothed again for she finds there a 'unison of many beauties, the river is very fine the Rock & Wood, Castle & Bridge grand Objects & the **Sugar Loaf** & **Skirrid** *(Mynydd Pen-y-fâl and Ysgyryd Fawr)* complete the delightful prospect'. She stays at the **Three Salmons**, where the ubiquitous itinerant Welsh harper entertains her and John, and where:

> . . . Mr. W. generously desir'd he would have as much Ale as he liked . . . we found when the Acct. was settled next morning our bard invoked his genius & regaled himself with 17 pots or Quarts of ale! *(3rd September 1802)*

The Three Salmons, Usk

She stops briefly at **Clytha Castle**, a large eye-catching folly erected in 1790 by its then owner, Mr Jones, in memory of his late and 'most excellent wife' Elizabeth, a grand-daughter of the second Duke of Devonshire. Sarah takes:

> . . . a complete survey of these fine grounds, the united gazebo and mausoleum to his late wife, & [we]were most hospitably entertained with the finest hothouse fruit by the pensive owner! He still mourns his lost companion, & an air of melancholy recollection pervaded the elegance displayed in both house & garden. *(4th September 1802)*

Abergavenny is Sarah's final stop on this tour. She stays at the Angel Inn where, ten years later, Ann Bletchley was to be so terrified by the French officers and the rats. It was the coaching inn for the town and Sarah finds there 'angels & ministers of grease, busy & perturbed spirits'. From here she climbs the nearby Skirrid or Holy Mountain. Folklore suggests that the great bite that appears to have been taken out of its side happened at the time of the Crucifixion. The reality – a landslip that occurred during the last Ice Age – is a little less fanciful. She also walks to **Coldbrook House**, where she has another outburst against neglectful owners. This time it is because the extensive land is 'all hastening to decay, while the wretched owner is seeking shelter from his Creditors who pursue him at every turn!' This is not yet her final tirade for she next travels to **Llanthony's** Augustinian priory, over '6 miles of the very worst road in the bottom of a ditch'. On her arrival, she laments that the owner 'should rase to the ground so magnificent a

The Angel Inn, Abergavenny

monument . . . if tired of the haunts of men . . . why not chuse a distant spot to make his residence, & leave this sublime object to . . . show his taste for the sublime & beautiful!' However her soul, which at the start of her tour had seemed so agitated, seems soothed by all she sees for the valley is:

> . . . admirably suited to the seclusion of a monastic life! The mountains which surround rear their russet fronts above the clouds! A few tall pines & firs are thinly scatter'd on their sides; & in the Vale a few distorted Hawthorns serve to shew the season when in the world all nature smiles with plenty! Here deep silence reigns & moping melancholy sits enthroned! No birds disturb their meditation with their cheerful notes! No human track across the field is traced! The Ewias alone murmurs as it glides & winds its narrow path, the never failing friend to man; the health preserving gift of God! Here stands the beauteous abbey. *(9th September 1802)*

From the peace of Llanthony, Sarah and John return to their 'comfortable Home highly delighted with our Tour, & grateful for the all the blessings & benefits we have enjoy'd for 6 delightful weeks of health, peace and Competence!', an example perhaps of the healing power of travel. Despite the problems of poor weather, tirades against irresponsible landlords, and disappointment with some of the architecture, Sarah's diary still brims over with pleasure and with a sense of her own good fortune in seeing such a beautiful country; a good fortune enhanced, I suspect, by a comfortable home life, good health, and above all a happy marriage.

These two early diarists write very differently – Frances Crewe dashed round north Wales and her diary reflects this; whilst Sarah Wilmot took time to savour south Wales and to sketch as well as to write – but what both these diarists share is an infectious enjoyment of all that they saw in the landscape and a real appreciation of the civility of the people they encountered.

Chapter 3

The Lady and her Companion:
the diaries of Millicent Bant,
companion to Lady Wilson, (1806, 1808, 1812)

*Fishguard is a miserable sea port. Lady Wilson determined to sleep here, the Road
being too bad and too far to reach Cardigan before dark, so to work she went, had the
only two Beds in the house aired, very well off for our Dinner, but not a drop of Wine.
Sent out Sophia and Coachman on a foraging party, to try their luck: sent them first
to the Doctor's, so-called here. Poor, miserable Creature, he had none; Parson of
course had none; enquired for the Lawyer, none resident; at last the Coachman saw
something like a poor Gentleman's House, Sophia knocked and begged a bottle of
Wine, saying whatever they chose should be paid for, and thanks also, as her Lady
was in great distress for some; the Boon was granted, and they returned triumphant,
Coachman bearing the prize in his hand.*

8th July 1808

* * *

Two very different – but equally indomitable – women made several visits
to Wales in the early nineteenth century. The first is a Lady, a widow who
clearly enjoyed her wine and would brook no opposition in tracking it
down. The second is her 'humble servant', the unmarried Millicent Bant, a
gentlewoman in reduced circumstances, who is the author of the diaries.
Three other characters also play minor parts: the coachman, and the maids,
Sophia and Margaret, shadowy figures about whom, as servants, nothing is
known. A good deal, however, is known about their employer, Lady
Wilson, born Jane Weller in May 1749. She was widely regarded as a beauty
and, when only eighteen, she attracted the attention and then the love of a
man over twice her age, Sir Thomas Spencer Wilson, a battle-scarred
veteran of campaigns in many parts of the world. The attraction between
them must have been both strong and immediate as they married within
weeks of meeting. The couple had four children, one of whom – also Jane –
had the misfortune to lose her first husband to an assassin: she had married
Spencer Perceval, the only British Prime Minister to have ever met such an
end.

For most of their married life, Jane and Sir Thomas lived at Charlton
House, a fine Jacobean mansion in Kent which had been inherited by Jane.
By the time of her husband's death, all four children were adults, leaving the
forty-nine year old Jane without a role as either wife or mother. Four years

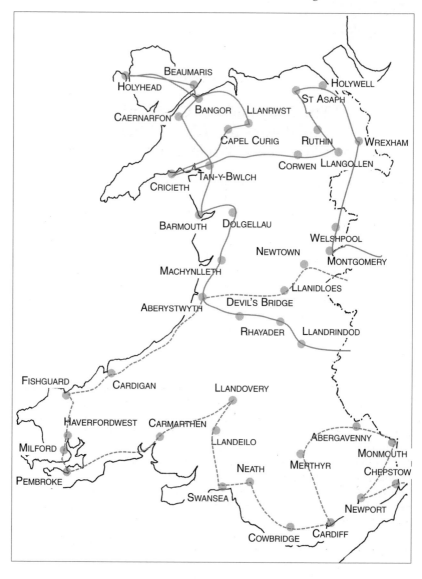

Lady Wilson and Millicent Bant.
1806: an extensive tour through mid and north Wales.
1808: an extensive tour through south and west Wales.
1812: A brief tour from Hay-on-Wye to Monmouth (no map).

later she was also replaced as mistress of **Charlton House** when her eldest son and his family moved in.

It was clear that Lady Wilson needed a new life. It began when she met and made friends with Millicent Bant, for the result of this friendship was indefatigable travelling, over a number of years, to almost every county in England, Scotland and Wales. Lady Wilson and her faithful companion began their travels in 1804 with an extensive tour in northern England and the Lake District, followed by Scotland in 1805. Their first visit to Wales was in 1806 when Lady Wilson would have been fifty-seven years of age. They visited Sussex later in the same year and Scotland in 1807; were back in Wales in 1808, Scotland again in 1809, and Wales again in 1812. Age did not seem to diminish Lady Wilson's travelling enthusiasm, for Millicent comments that Lady Wilson's passion for travelling annually 'to different parts of England, Scotland and Wales in search of the various beauties [with] which Nature and Art have so abundantly stored this happy country and its sister Kingdom and Dependencies increases with her age'.

From what Millicent writes about her employer, Lady Wilson appears to be autocratic, bossy, and something of a drinker. Yet this does not do her justice at all. She was scientifically knowledgeable, and was said to be able to name all of the thousands of mineral specimens she collected. In the diaries she can sometimes sound critical about the poor that she meets, although she was in fact adored and respected by the poor in her home area. When news of the end of the Napoleonic wars was received, she gave a roast beef and plum pudding dinner to three hundred poor of the parish at Charlton House; and when she died in 1818, nearly all her tenants attended her funeral, for although 'she was one of the gentry, and wealthy, her relationship with the lower classes was without affectation'.

Millicent gives the impression of being middle-aged, serious and at times waspish. Her diary is full of seemingly factual information about what she sees, much of it no doubt gleaned from the guide books of the time, but these dry facts are of far less interest than her comments on the less well-known places they visit, the inns they stay in and their various adventures en route. Millicent is endlessly curious about what she sees as they dash on, day after day, through the Welsh countryside and towns, with a particular fascination for church monuments and grand houses. She can be scathing, probably justifiably at that time, about the inns, and ambivalent about the grand houses, and her throwaway remarks about people and living conditions, jumbled in with comments on the picturesque nature of the country, can sometimes seem critical and unsympathetic. Yet despite all this, her lively and interesting comments provide another glimpse into life in early nineteenth-century Wales.

Millicent and Lady Wilson leave Charlton for Wales on 3rd of July 1806. During their six-week holiday they travel nearly every day and cover a vast mileage in the carriage. Their visit does not, however, start very auspiciously. Having passed through **Llandrindod Wells** (*Llandrindod*) without stopping to sample the famous medicinal waters, Lady Wilson sends the coachman to see whether the nearby **Water Break Its Neck** waterfall is worth visiting. He has a mile's tramp on his Ladyship's behalf and returns to tell them that, as there is little water in it, they need not bother to make the detour to it. The journey to **Rhayader** (*Rhaeadr*), where they spend their first night in Wales, is frightening, as part of the road is 'over a very steep hill, with a precipice on one side'.

As they drive along, fearful that the carriage might go over the edge and the whole party be dashed to pieces, the driver regales them with stories of carriages that had met such a fate. On hearing these tales 'her Ladyship's maid was so much alarmed . . . she immediately jumpt off the Dickey'. Millicent was not much less frightened, yet she is still able to observe one of the local inhabitants doing her washing by 'beating her Cloaths with a Mallet upon a Wooden form by the Riverside'. Rhayader proves to be a 'dirty hole' and, to make matters worse, there is 'no wine to be had'.

They are on the go again next morning. It takes them eight hours to travel the nineteen miles to **Devil's Bridge** (*Pontarfynach*). It must have been hot, tiring and uncomfortable jolting along yet another precipitous road, so narrow that 'in many parts, Carriages cannot pass each other'. As soon as they arrive, they walk to the famous Devil's Bridge falls, which 'her Ladyship thinks infinitely superior to any she has seen in Cumberland in point of Height, Water & Scenery'. These 300 ft high falls are famous both for their beauty and the bridges that span them. When Millicent and Lady Wilson were there, only two of the current three bridges existed: the first, reputed to have been built by the Devil, is in fact a medieval bridge; whilst the second was built in 1753 to take horse-drawn vehicles. The waterfalls might have impressed, but the inn – the **Hafod Arms** – does not, as the beds 'are horribly stinking'. Next day they visit **Hafod**:

> . . . the celebrated seat of Mr. Jones [Johnes] which has had a great deal too much said of it in the Books. House neat, with a few good paintings, one room is beautifully furnished with tapestry; Library is a handsome circular building, with a gallery round it, supported by eight marble pillars, in the ante library is some very fine painted glass; no admission into the Conservatory or Flower Garden. A violent shower prevented our walking in the grounds, except to the smallest waterfall, which is extremely picturesque & pretty. Lady Wilson said she did not like the celebrated place so well as Foxley & many other places. *(11th July 1806)*

Hafod was in fact one of the highlights of any tour to mid-Wales during the late eighteenth and early nineteenth centuries, and many artists, writers and tourists made special journeys to see it. It was the creation of Thomas Johnes and, in its heyday, was considered to be amongst the finest picturesque estates in Britain. The garden was intended to be a rural paradise with sculptures, caves, bridges and fantastic vistas; whilst the house contained an impressive collection of fine art. Paradise on earth, however, is elusive, and Thomas Johnes' own particular one ended, first with a fire in 1807 and then with the death of his beloved only daughter Mariamne in 1811. Although Johnes rebuilt Hafod after the fire, and there was a later remodelling, the glory days were over; and when the house was demolished in 1956 another little piece of paradise was lost for ever. In comparing it unfavourably with Foxley, which she had visited en route to Wales, Lady Wilson is showing off her impeccable 'picturesque' credentials, for Foxley in Herefordshire was the home of Uvedale Price, best known for his *Essays on the Picturesque*, and Price and Johnes would have known each other well.

Millicent and Lady Wilson leave Devil's Bridge without regret, and journey on to **Aberystwyth**, 'a miserable town . . . meat & everything else very nasty, very slight remains of the castle, a pleasant walk round it & a glorious view of the Bay of Cardigan and the surrounding mountains'. After a brief stop they ride on to **Machynlleth** and then have an 'extremely beautiful' drive to Dolgellau. Millicent is bowled over by the descent into Dolgellau which is 'beautiful beyond description', but the town is 'beastly, there is but one Inn, which is surrounded with Pig Sties, nothing to be got but fried Mutton Chops, might as well eat a piece of old Goat, nothing made it bearable but a Welsh harper, who was playing the whole of the dinner time'.

Like Frances Crewe before them, Millicent and Lady Wilson travel along the shores of the Mawddach estuary to Barmouth, 'so irregularly built . . . that the windows of one house not uncommonly look over the Chimnies of another. We could not avoid observing the number of Pigs lying in every corner of the Streets'. The inn is full and Millicent and her Ladyship are obliged to sit in a '*public* room where Victuals hard to be got, & when it came not eatable'.

They leave Barmouth for **Tan y Bwlch** and the **Oakeley Arms Hotel**, which had been built by the Oakeleys, prominent local quarry owners, for the increasing numbers of travellers coming to Wales. Millicent reports with relief that, 'after seven hours & three quarters drive over a perfect Sea of Mountains', they have been transported from a 'pigsty to a palace . . . a perfect Paradise'. It is such a paradise that they stay for two days before driving even further into the grandeur of north Wales, Millicent clearly enjoying the scenery and finding 'Snowdon a fine fellow'. Paradise, however, does not greet them at the **Caernarfon Hotel** in **Caernarfon**, where they are 'first saluted with "no beds" but after a little talking gained admittance. Inn good in every respect except the Women Waiters, alias Kent Street Cinder Wenches'. This was probably a reference to the dirtiness of the waitresses, as cinder wenches raked ashes for living, with the Kent Street cinder wenches perhaps being particularly dirty examples of the species. At last Millicent has found a town to her taste. It is 'large & handsome' and 'the castle though a complete ruin [is] not debased with any modern architecture or cottage within its walls . . . [it] was built by Edward the First and by the united efforts of the Peasants executed in the space of one year'.

The following day, Millicent and Lady Wilson cross by ferry over the

Menai Strait to **Anglesey** (*Ynys Môn*). They visit **Plas Newydd** where Millicent is impressed by its grandeur. 'The house is modern, large . . . hall & dining parlour Gothic, latter large enough to dine one Hundred persons, the Drawing Room is hung with yellow painted Taffety, a present from the Queen'. From here they travel across Anglesey to **Holyhead** (*Caergybi*) but, as they have now been travelling every day for well over two weeks, Lady Wilson's temper is becoming a little frayed; she gets into a 'great passion with the servants' and only pays them half their fee, which is all she feels their service justifies. At Holyhead, where people are hurrying to catch the Dublin Packet boat, the 'inn is in an uproar', but nothing like the uproar they meet next day when they visit **Parys Mountain** which, at that time, was Europe's most important copper mine.

Here Millicent and Lady Wilson find themselves in 'a most curious, interesting, awful & infernal place . . . the sulphurous stench and thundering noise from the blasting of the rocks gives one a faint Idea what Mount Vesuvius must be'. So fantastic were the mines considered to be that they became part of the Welsh Grand Tour, with the artists of the day delighting in painting the miners as they swung over the cliff face extracting the copper. Today the remains of the mines, looking rather like a lunar landscape, are silent and somewhat eerie.

Leaving this 'infernal place' Millicent and Lady Wilson travel to **Beaumaris** (*Biwmares*), where they find that, in their inn, there is to be some sort of show in which 'a young female Roscius was to perform that evening a Wonderful Child, in Lady W's opinion & ought to be encouraged . . . this Child is not yet seven years of age'. Who this young genius was remains a mystery, but the late eighteenth century saw a vogue for child actors, of whom 'the young Roscius', William Henry West, was the most famous. Millicent does not say whether this young artiste lives up to expectations, for her diary is much more concerned with the fact that they are overtaken by inclement weather and are unable to cross back to the mainland for three days.

Millicent's diary is full of woe. They are 'out of patience' and there is 'dish of grumbling'. Despite this they walk on the beach; visit **Baron Hill**, home of the powerful Viscount Lord Bulkeley, which Millicent finds to be in an attractive setting; and look at a collection of stuffed birds owned by a Miss Meyrick, member of another prominent Anglesey family. When they finally get away and are back on the mainland they are still relentless in their pursuit of curiosities. They go to see 'the flint mill where they grind the flints for glazing China Ware . . . [and] an Oil & Paint Mill, which we did not go into as Lady Wilson was afraid of the noise'; admire Lord Penrhyn's slate quarry, a 'very curious scene', and then go on to see his home at **Penrhyn Castle** 'grounds beautiful, stables the best fitted up of any in Europe, slated inside & out, also an elegant hot & cold sea bath, slated with handsome furnished apartments for dressing & undressing, and a very pretty cottage and Chapel'.

From here they continue to travel through north Wales having, 'at **Aber**, quite the best drest Dinner & civilest landlord of any we have met with on our journey'. They drive over **Penmaenmawr**, where Millicent is disappointed as she finds 'the rise of the hill is not so steep as the Hill at Blackheath'. At **Conwy**, Millicent, with her love of detail, describes a delightful monument in the church which has 'a curious figure of a Woman carved on a pavement stone, with five Children cut out, towards the Top of her Petticoat, three on one side, & two on the other'. She explores the castle, the town and the 'beautiful objects in all directions', commenting in particular on the Elizabethan house 'now inhabited by poor families . . . adorned after the fantastical fashion of the times in which it was erected, the Roof is singularly carved, and the front decorated with the Arms of England, with several Crests of Birds & Beads'. This fine house, **Plas Mawr**, built by the merchant Robert Wynn, still stands proudly in the centre of Conwy, and is a perfectly preserved example of one of Britain's finest Elizabethan town houses.

From Conwy, Millicent and her Ladyship go to **Llanrwst**, where Millicent's diary goes into breathless overload with one theme being so hotly followed by another that, rather like her travels, each thing seems to run into the next. There is the bridge allegedly (but probably not) built by Inigo Jones in 1636 where 'two men stand on the Bridge who by striking the battlements over the Middle Arch shake the Bridge & pick your Pockets'; and the church which is 'extremely old, many curious old monuments, some of them with curious carved screens; and the stone coffin of Llewellyn the Great'. The 'curious carved screen' is probably the rood screen taken there from the nearby **Maenan Abbey** when it was suppressed at the Dissolution of the monasteries; whilst the stone casing of Llywelyn's sarcophagus is still there. The sarcophagus itself disappeared after the Dissolution, and the final resting place of Llywelyn is unknown.

They return to the inn, 'expecting to find a good dinner, but only half we ordered was brought to the table, her Ladyship in a great rage docked the Bill'. They set off after dinner to go to **Capel Curig** for the night, but as there is 'only one Bed to be had'; Millicent was 'obliged to have one made on the sofa . . . I thought myself fortunate in getting that, as many others who came after us were obliged to sleep on the floor'. Next day Millicent and Lady Wilson have what must have been a long and tiring day. They travel in their carriage to **Cricieth** on the **Llyn Peninsula**, passing through scenery that is 'truly awful and sublime . . . many Mountains which were more terrific than Penmaenmawr'. When they arrive at Cricieth, Millicent seems to be deceived by some exaggerated claims of the local people, for she comments that although this town 'was formerly the largest in Britain, the whole that now remains are a few miserable Huts and the Ruins of the Castle'. Cricieth was indeed a Welsh town with a thirteenth-century Welsh castle (even though briefly taken over by Edward I) and it was important, but 'the largest in Britain' is definitely an exaggeration. Yet, despite the rigours of this long day they leave the inn by 6 a.m. in order to see the sunrise on the nearby **Ogwen Pool**, arriving 'to the minute to see the Reflection of the Mountains in the

Glass Pool . . . the beauty of the Scene cannot be described, the Storm the Day before had given full force to the Waterfall which was extremely fine'.

From here Millicent and her Ladyship turn their heads and their horses back towards England. As they travel, in contrast to her earlier comments about Lady Wilson's testiness with servants, Millicent comments on the fact that, as Lady Wilson is 'not spending her Money fast enough, [she] is in the habit of giving Beggars Dollars, instead of penny pieces'. These 'dollars' were silver pieces of eight stamped with the head of George II, and were legitimate currency from 1797 until 1821, a period when the fear of invasion by the French was so real that people wanted the security of holding their assets in gold or silver and not paper money.

They stop several times on their homeward journey. At **Cernioge**, after another hard day's travelling, they find yet another 'miserable inn'. At the time this coaching inn, standing alone on a rather bleak road, was so well known that the name Cernioge appeared on the milestones in the area and even today observant travellers can find some of these old milestones still gracing the roadside. Millicent and Lady Wilson are up again by dawn and on the road by 6 a.m., finding the whole country to be 'a perfect paradise'. They stop at Bala for dinner; take a drive round **Llyn Tegid** and then go on to Corwen where they retire gratefully to bed.

They have now been travelling for nearly a month, yet their energy for exploring antiquities appears undiminished, for the next day, the 3rd of

Milestone marking the isolated coaching inn at Cernioge

August, they travel to Llangollen where they walk up to Plas Newydd, a 'pretty little interesting place'; and where Millicent notes that the church has one 'thing particular . . . a curious ceiling, and one handsome Monument, very dirty, as usual . . . the town is filled with beggars'. They expect to leave Llangollen very speedily, but back at their inn they are informed 'by the Landlord with the greatest sang froid imaginable, that he had sent [the horses] with another carriage'. This means a frustrating delay of six hours before being able to ride on to **Ruthin** *(Rhuthun)* which Millicent finds is 'a sweet pretty place . . . extremely clean . . . the **White Lion** . . . a clean Inn & civil people'. She is so entranced by the town that she advises 'all those who have small fortunes to retire to Ruthin'. However, she does not take her own advice, as she and Lady Wilson rush on to **Denbigh** *(Dinbych)*, only stopping to look at the 'very good painted glass, subject the Rock of Jesse' at **Llanrhaeadr** church and **St Dyfnog's Well**, 'once famous for curing the Rheumatism, now a mere ruin, with a pleasant walk round it; caught in a violent shower of Rain, completely wetted, dryed ourselves in a Public House'.

As well as being interested in all that she sees, Millicent also clearly enjoys collecting information about local customs, as the next sentence in her diary, completely unrelated to the previous topic, reads that 'it is the Custom of this part of the Country every Christmas morning at five to illuminate their churches'. Having dried off, they visit nearby **Lleweni Hall**, a large, mainly medieval, house that was almost entirely demolished ten years later, making Millicent's brief description of yet another 'lost house' particularly interesting. She writes that it is:

> . . . a fine old house, Hall fine with curious arched roof, in it is a complete armoury, and a collection of Stuffed Birds, and a few old Pictures. At one end is a gallery with a handsome Organ; Drawing Room hung with Tapestry, Subject from Telemachus, from the front you have a fine view of Denbigh Town & Castle. *(4th August 1806)*

The 'curious roof' was a hammerbeam one; when the house was demolished the organ was installed in St Hilary's church in Denbigh, whilst the 'few old pictures' were dispersed. In Denbigh, Millicent grumbles that 'the Town is a very bad one, not a good House in it, the castle not worth looking at'. Rather than staying in such a 'bad' town, Millicent and her Ladyship journey on to **St Asaph** *(Llanelwy)*, where they stay for three days in 'a very middling inn, amused the whole time with clapping of doors enough to distract one'.

After this brief respite from travelling they are back in the carriage, with their next stop being the well at **Holywell** *(Treffynnon)*. Once considered one of the seven wonders of Wales, it is dedicated to St Winefride, whose head was cut off, but miraculously put back on by her uncle. At that moment, according to legend, a healing spring gushed forth on the spot. When Millicent saw the well it was still producing 'every minute Night & Day, one hundred Tons of Water . . . said to cure several disorders; it Boils up with great impetuosity out of a Rock and is formed into a beautiful bath, the Roof supported by Pillars . . . exquisitely carved in Stone'. Today, although a shadow of its former self, it is the only holy well in Wales to have remained in continuous use as a place of pilgrimage since its foundation.

From here Millicent and Lady Wilson visit **Erddig**, which they find to be 'well furnished with Old & Modern furniture, several Old Cabinets, some good China and family Pictures, by far the best house we have seen as yet, Grounds extensive, well laid out with many remarkable trees'. From this fine house they move on to the excitement of the modern in both industry and civil engineering. First they visit the **Bersham Ironworks**:

> . . . Mr Wilkinson's Foundry; went over the whole works, there were many very curious Wheels, saw them roll the Iron into sheets and cast the Leaden Pipes three feet long which are after drawn to 10 feet; also saw the Immense Boilers for the Steam Engine, they come to three Hundred pounds each, they much resemble the Welsh haystacks. *(11th August 1806)*

Yet Bersham was already in decline when Millicent and Lady Wilson toured its wonders and it ceased manufacturing only four years later. They then drive to the recently opened **Pontcysyllte aqueduct** which, built to carry what is now the Llangollen canal over the river Dee, was, at 126 feet above the river, nick-named the 'stream in the sky'. Millicent, no doubt copying out her facts from a guide book, describes it in detail:

Bersham Ironworks: *Drawing of the West Works*
by John Westway Rowe, c. 1790.

> [It] extends 388 feet and consists of 19 arches each 45 feet in the span and the addition of 10 feet Six of Iron work at each end, in continuation & conveys the Water 1003 feet in a cast Iron trough 11 feet 8 inches broad; we walked over the Top, from it is a beautiful view of the Vale of the Dee, altogether it is a fine piece of Architecture, it may well be one of the Wonders of Wales. *(11th August 1806)*

From these technological wonders, they return to their exploration of castles, stopping at **Chirk**, which is 'kept in thorough repair'; and then **Powis**, with which Millicent is ambivalently impressed. She describes it at length, but feels that the picture gallery has been 'spoiled by modernizing . . . [and] contains not many Pictures, few of them good'. Powis was once owned by Clive of India, and it is not surprising therefore to find that Millicent is intrigued by the 'Model of an Elephant, with two Men upon it, the whole in complete armour, the Tusks are cut off, and in their places are placed two long swords'. Nevertheless in the older parts of the castle there are 'many good Pictures, Cabinets, Tapestry, Busts &c.'

They stay overnight in nearby **Welshpool** (*Y Trallwng*), and then visit **Llanfair Caereinion**, which they find 'the prettiest little market town in Wales, beautifully situated on a Hanging hill, with a fine River running at the bottom'. They breakfast at the coaching inn at **Cann Office**, where, ever interested in history, they learn that there is 'a Roman encampment, and a Tumulus, which the Landlord intends soon to explore', and finally, before leaving for England, visit **Montgomery** (*Trefaldwyn*), where they walk to the remains of the castle.

Despite the discomfort of many of the inns, the long, slow drives over bad roads, and Millicent's critical comments about much that she sees, both women clearly enjoyed their visit, for they return to Wales in 1808, this time to the south, setting out in late May. Even before they reach the Welsh border, they have an adventure caused by inebriated drivers:

> . . . who were incapable of governing the Horses, which ran away at a great speed down a steep Hill; fortunately, there were no obstructions, but the Banks on either side of the road were very steep and we were repeatedly dashed with great violence against them. At one time the Roof of the coach was within three feet of the Ground. Thank God!, the carriage righted, the front horse having got entangled in the Traces, and one of the front Wheels coming in contact with a foot Bridge at a Cottage Door, the further progress of the coach was stopt, and we luckily escaped injury, sustaining only a violent fright at the peril to which we had been exposed. *(29th May 1808)*

Their plan is to take the Wye tour but, before setting out by boat, they take a land trip to **Goodrich Castle**, which is 'easy of access and a very fine picturesque Ruin . . . found two Village Nymphs taking views of the castle, who quizzed us Butterfly Catchers' – the image of the fifty-nine year old

Goodrich castle (Sarah Wilmot, 1802)

Lady Wilson and her rather serious companion dashing about in their voluminous clothes with their butterfly nets is a wonderful one. Millicent, ever tenacious in her exploration of antiquities, inspects the church, 'which is very neat, contains only one Ancient Monument'.

They finally set out on their river tour after breakfast on the 31st of May, but are 'deprived of the pleasure we anticipated to have enjoyed in our aquatic excursion by a Thunderstorm'. Millicent lists the various official viewpoints that tourists are meant to admire, and describes the handsome white marble monument opposite Coldwell rocks 'in memory of a young Gentleman sixteen years of age, who . . . being a good swimmer went into the river to bathe, he came out, and at his Father's Request, went in again, got into the middle of the stream, and sunk to rise no more'. This memorial ends with the instructions that anyone in similar difficulties will find that 'apparatus and directions for their application by the Humane Society, for the saving of persons apparently drowned, are lodged at the church of Coldwell'. The only trouble with this well-meaning piece of information is that there is not, nor has there ever been, a church at Coldwell. Ever interested in the minutiae of what she sees, Millicent notes the 'water docks that grow in abundance on the river banks' and that 'the poor people were gathering the Leaves to boil for their hogs'.

They stop overnight at Monmouth, and then continue sailing down the Wye finding, as Sarah Wilmot did, that Tintern Abbey is 'quite perfect'. At Chepstow, Millicent and Lady Wilson take a stroll round the church, remarking on its 'Saxon' features and admiring the major monuments. In the evening they manage to walk half of the celebrated paths at Piercefield and also have the 'good fortune to get a peep at the house . . . a handsome modern structure, well situated for views . . . in the hall ten handsome Scagliola [plasterwork designed to imitate marble] pillars, the rest of the Apartments handsomely furnished'.

The following day they explore **Caldicot Castle**, which Millicent says has 'many vestiges that prove it to have been formerly a very stately and magnificent building . . . the situation of this Edifice is very singular, being built in a meadow, which is contrary to the general custom of erecting castles in elevated places'. They are then appalled by what they feel has been sheer vandalism, for they find that at **Caerwent** the fine Roman pavement:

> . . . no longer existed. Time's corroding hand had not effected its destruction, but the tasteless Proprietor of the once beautiful work of the Ancients had caused the building which had been erected over it to be pulled down, and left [it] to be spoiled and destroyed by the rude hands of depredators, desirous of being possessed of a portion of the antique relic, or ignorant of its beauty. To be deprived of a sight of this rarity of ancient art and workmanship by such means was the source of great regret to us, and the disappointment we sustained excited our mental execration of the being who had so negligently, nay, almost wantonly given up to destruction that thing which in the possession of an antiquarian would have been prized as a gem of infinite value. *(2nd June 1808)*

Millicent, unlike Sarah Wilmot before her, finds the inn at Newport 'very good & the people very civil'; whilst Tredegar House is 'a fine old place'. From here Millicent and Lady Wilson journey along the Usk valley where Millicent makes a very odd comment, for she writes that the Monmouthshire hills are 'more numerous and steep than any in north Wales' – odd because, having seen the north Wales mountains, she must have known that these hills, though lovely, are much lower. When they arrive in Monmouth,

Caldicot castle (Sarah Wilmot, 1802)

Millicent turns from descriptions of places to people. On Sunday morning
Lady Wilson goes alone to church where she meets:

> . . . a specimen of Welsh hospitality to strangers. Lady Wilson . . . was
> first in the Pew & seated herself on a small Cushion of which there were
> three. A Dame in Pattens with her two daughters soon entered . . .
> seeing her Ladyship on one of the cushions and probably in the corner
> usually occupied by herself she looked as black as thunder, pulled out
> an Hassock, and down she flounced. When the sentences began Lady
> Wilson got up and turning towards the Parson did not suppose what
> was going on behind her, but when she set down, found her Cushion
> was flown. In the Evening I went with her Ladyship. The Dame was
> going to play me the same trick, but being on the watch, I turned round,
> caught her in the act and she relinquished her prize. *(5th June 1808)*

Leaving Monmouth for **Crickhowell** *(Crycywel)*, they stop at Coldbrook
House, whose neglectful owner had so incensed Sarah Wilmot. Millicent
does not seem to have any of the same qualms, for she enjoys 'the Hall and
two drawing rooms, several good Family Pictures, and fine Bronzes, two
very handsome mahogany stands, supporting two marble slabs, the Legs
represented Greyhounds, exquisitely carved'. She also finds their next stop,
Abergavenny, a 'clean, neat town'. She visits the church with its 'eleven
curious monuments': regarded today as one of the outstanding series of
medieval monuments in the British Isles, they are but one of the delights of
this former Benedictine priory.

As they journey on, they stop at an inn to water the horses, and hear a
melancholy story about a neighbour of the landlord's who 'had just hung
herself, having been for some time in a melancholy state. Her husband was
gone to market, and a neighbour on passing by saw her hanging. Suicide is
so common in Wales that they think nothing of it'. Although people were far
more used to death as part of life than we are today, suicide was still a
criminal offence, and Millicent's casual attitude to what must have seemed a
shocking event seems odd. Indeed it is curious how often the diarists
juxtapose notes about poverty, death or some deep distress for people next to
descriptions of landscape. Millicent is no exception, as in her next sentence
she says 'the scenery today is picturesque in the extreme'.

At Brecon they enjoy the 'curious old place' that is now the cathedral; as
well as the Captain's walk, so called because the French prisoners of war who
were held in Brecon during the Napoleonic wars used to exercise there. She
also describes another case of vandalism when 'a gentleman of considerable
property . . . discovered on his estate a Roman Bath and Hypocaust, and
some beautiful pavement but he, being a perfect Goth, had it destroyed
because the people made a path across his fields'.

From Brecon, they travel along 'a very bad road, barely passable' to
Merthyr Tydfil, 'a singular, large, odd built town, Inn much better than we
expected. Our Dinner was drest today by a Turnspit. This Town is chiefly

inhabited by the Workmen employed in the extensive Iron Works for which [it] is so famous'. Indeed they were, for Merthyr Tydfil was, at that time, rapidly becoming the foremost iron producer in the world and was already the largest town in Wales. The workers lived in cramped and squalid conditions, although their masters, who lived in grand houses akin to palaces, often lived cheek by jowl with their noisy, smelly ironworks.

Cardiff is Millicent's next stop and from here they make an excursion to Caerphilly Castle. Unlike Sarah Wilmot, Millicent seems untouched by this grand castle, finding the bridge at **Pontypridd** far more fascinating. At that time it would still have been famous as the largest single span bridge in Europe, and have seemed to them yet another wonder of the scientific age in which they were living. They walk about a half a mile to see the salmon leap at the **Berw waterfall**, but find it 'not worth the trouble' and then ride to **Taff's Well**, a mineral well famous for treating 'Rheumatism and other complaints; the poor People flock in great numbers to it'.

Back at Cardiff, they enjoy visits to the castle and **Llandaf Cathedral** before going on to St Donat's, with its church, set in a 'sequestered dale' below the castle, being the 'most curious and ancient place' she has ever seen. Millicent continues to be fascinated by details at the less popular tourist sites she visits and, at nearby **Llantrithyd**, she writes about the 'curious chimney pieces . . . the drawing room a coved ceiling in squares, the knots are ornamented with Coats of Arms, and the ceiling contains the Arms of all the Gentleman in the County of Glamorgan'. Millicent was lucky to have seen this, for this grand house, once one of the great sixteenth-century houses of Wales, is now a ruin.

St Donat's (Sarah Wilmot, 1802)

Next day, having slept at Cowbridge, they are up early and off before breakfast to see the ruins of **Old Beaupre Castle** which had been well recommended to them by their landlord. Despite the fact that these substantial medieval ruins were – and still are – spectacular, Millicent is not impressed. They go back to Cowbridge for breakfast and then, undeterred by this disappointment, set off again to visit **Dunraven**, 'a modern castle' which indeed it was, as the medieval manor house had only just been replaced by a Gothic mansion. As grand castles go, however, it had a short life as it was demolished in 1963 and now only the gardens remain.

At **St Bride's** church Millicent is amused by a monument to a John Wyndham and his wife who died in 1697 and 1698 respectively, 'a man and Woman, half length, stuck up in a pulpit as if talking to each other; they are painted in colours, making altogether a very ridiculous appearance'. She also manages to make a brief visit to the Benedictine **Ewenni Priory** which, although even then in ruins, was nevertheless the most complete and impressive Norman ecclesiastical building in Glamorgan. By contrast with this evocative place, the church Millicent sees next day at **Llantrisant** is:

> . . . the most tatterdemalion place we ever saw. Roof nearly gone, Pews and pavement all to pieces; only one figure remaining, a very curious wooden one, made of flesh and blood. It stood on a stand six feet from the Ground, tolling the Bell with both hands, the most curious thing we have seen in Wales. *(11th June 1808)*

Millicent then returns to Cowbridge for the night, where she comments on the pigsties which are 'remarkable for their form and strength, being built of stone, circular, [with] a stone Conical Roof, ending in a point. The Breed of Pigs the ugliest and [most] ill-made we ever saw'. From Cowbridge Millicent and Lady Wilson visit **Kenfig Pool** where she is metaphorically sucked into some of the many myths that have become attached to it. This 'very great curiosity' was, she says, 'produced by an Earthquake, which then threw down the Borough town of Cynfig'. The more pedestrian explanation is that the pool came into being when the drainage of the area was blocked by the formation of the coastal dune system in prehistoric times, so that the dunes gradually engulfed the old borough town.

Millicent is far more impressed with Margam than was Sarah Wilmot, and she describes the greenhouses and famous Orangery at length, but she is singularly unimpressed with Lord Vernon's house at **Briton Ferry** (*Llansawel*). This is another house that has been demolished but it was, at that time, popular with 'picturesque' tourists. Millicent is rather scathing about it, finding it 'not worth notice, grounds in very bad order, but picturesque and pretty on the banks of the river'. From Neath, where they stop overnight, Millicent and Lady Wilson explore the **Vale of Neath** (*Glyn Neath*), another essential stop for the picturesque tourist in search of the sublime; this time grand waterfalls instead of mountains. But for them the experience is not a happy one.

They stay at **Pont-nedd-fechan**, at the head of the valley, in a 'beastly Inn, more Beastly Woman, and most Beastly Breakfast! Bread full of dirt and feathers. After all this dirt and filth were not able to see more than one waterfall out of seven'. She doesn't say why this is so, but most of the falls require walking, some of it difficult, to get to them, and Lady Wilson is unable to climb up to **Aberdulais**, the one fall they do see. Although this waterfall had been generating energy for various kinds of industry since 1584, the area was still deeply rural and very picturesque. It was only later in the eighteenth century that industry began to mar the vale, but the wonderful waterfalls are still there for today's picturesque tourist to see. It is a relief to them to return to their 'indifferent' inn at Neath, which now seems like 'a perfect palace to the hovel we had just left'.

Millicent and Lady Wilson travel, as did Sarah Wilmot, past the copper works and on to Swansea, from where they visit **Penrice**, the 'new' mansion belonging to Thomas Mansel Talbot who had chosen this 'most romantic spot' when he decided to move from Margam. Millicent comments that 'the house is modern, nothing in it worth notice, but a few good pictures and one mosaic chimney piece, extremely beautiful . . . the view from the house . . . exceeding fine. The grounds are very pretty'. Penrice, on the **Gower Peninsula**, is only about ten miles from Swansea, but such was the roughness of the road that their travelling time was seven hours in all – a long day's drive for a disappointing house. As a sea mist prevents them travelling next day, they visit the **Cambrian pottery**, which was the most famous of the Swansea potteries, and where they find the 'different articles of superior quality and more genteel than those sold at Christie's'.

From Swansea they travel inland to Llandeilo, again stopping to admire various old houses. There is **Taliaris**, which has 'nothing in it except one good old ceiling, Dairy very large, quite in the farming stile, uncommonly sweet and clean'; **Edwinsford**, now a derelict mansion but then 'an old house, with four very ancient ceilings, one painted, and a few remains of the original furniture'; whilst **Glynhir**, home of the DuBoisson family, of Huguenot extraction, had its very own waterfall, the highest in Carmarthenshire. They have better luck with this waterfall than those in the Vale of Neath, as they are accompanied to it by none less than Mr DuBoisson, finding it 'beautifully situated in a deep dark wooded Glen, of easy access, through nice walks . . . very pretty and picturesque, well worth the attention of the traveller and paid us well for the bad Roads'. They continue to be relentless in their pursuit of fine houses, for they also visit **Middleton Hall**, 'a good modern house . . . grounds well laid out and watered. The views from both fronts very fine; altogether the prettiest place we have yet seen'; dash on to **Golden Grove**, the grand country seat of the wealthy Cawdors, and finally see **Dinefwr Castle**, home of the almost equally wealthy Dynevors. At the former, Millicent writes, the 'grounds contain nothing worth notice'; whilst at the latter they find that the house 'has nothing in it, except five carved ceilings. Park extremely large . . . and finely wooded'.

At Llandeilo, where the cattle market is held in the two churchyards, all is 'confusion, the Carriage completely surrounded by Cattle, Men, Women, Horses &c.; could not stir an inch. The Inn turned out better than we expected; people very civil'. At this point in her journal Millicent includes a couple of incidents which seem to have got out of order in her writing, but that she clearly wants to remember. The first is about a 'specimen of humanity – a poor old Woman, 90 years of age, mother to the Woman of the Inn, who died lately, sits from morning to night, turning the spit by an immense fire, not a foot from it'; whilst the second was of an awful sight seen on the previous day:

> . . . the funeral of a Man and his Wife who both died of a fever within half an hour of each other. A large concourse of people attended it, in no manner of order, nor any in mourning, some of them bare headed, singing before the coffins, which were carried abreast of each other on Biers. The coffins were without Palls, not made with lids, but covers. *(20th June 1808)*

From Llandeilo they go on to Carmarthen 'through a perfect garden . . . a very fine day, and of course a beautiful drive'. Millicent shows off her literary knowledge as she comments that Sir Richard Steele, author of *The Conscious Lovers* (though perhaps better known as an essayist and founder of the *Tatler* magazine), lived in the house opposite their inn and was buried in the church. From here Millicent turns her attention from fine houses to fine castles. At **Kidwelly** (*Cydweli*) she is fascinated by the remains of the 'soldiers ovens and bake house . . . and the Brewhouse [where] the holes remain through which they used to pour the beer into coolers'; at **Llansteffan**, although it was too steep for Lady Wilson, Millicent climbs to the top of the tower, but finds it too misty for a view; Laugharne she finds a 'fine old ruin', whilst **Manorbier** – the birthplace, about 1146, of Gerald of Wales – 'looks well at a distance, being much covered with ivy'.

They stop overnight in Tenby, where they drive on the sands and where Millicent, ever observant, notes that the 'rocks are curiously encrusted with a variety of shells and sea weeds'. Their next stop is Pembroke, where the **Green Dragon** is 'a very good inn', although Millicent finds Pembroke itself 'a nasty straggling ill-built town . . . [with] scarce a decent house'. She and Lady Wilson visit **Orielton**, a grand private house, where there are 'as many windows as days in the year . . . nothing particular in the House . . . in one of the closets which had become very offensive, by taking down a panel, the Housekeeper killed one hundred and nineteen Bats, some of them had three young ones at their teats'. In fact, Millicent had her facts wrong again, for there are not nearly as many windows as she states, although there are enough panes of glass for 'days in a year'. The bats are still there and now, of course, a protected species. Next day they visit **Stack Rocks**, which are:

> . . . covered with Eligoos, and other Sea Birds, which remain for three months. If disturbed when sitting, they take their Egg up in one foot

and fly to another part of the Cliff. When the danger is past, they take it back again, and finish their incubations. When the breeding season is over they swim away with their young on their backs, some of them carry two, but most of them one. Their numbers are immense, and when swimming darken the Sea. They make a great noise and send a powerful stench on shore; altogether a most curious and beautiful sight. *(2nd July 1808)*

The 'eligoos' were probably guillemots, for another name for Stack rocks is the 'Elegug rocks' which is derived from 'gwylog', the Welsh word for guillemot. Millicent must have been listening to some humorous folklore, for these guillemots do not behave as she describes. They may shuffle their eggs on their feet if disturbed, but they do not carry them, and in the water the young swim alongside their parents. Millicent obviously tries the holy water at the nearby **St Govan's** tiny hermit cell, for she finds it 'dirty, and of little taste, it is famous for the King's Evil [scrofula] and other complaints'. Here Millicent's curiosity about all that she sees is transferred to geology as she notes 'a curious excavation in the Rock, taking the form of a skeleton, also two stones which, when struck, sound like a bell'. One of the perforations in the cliff, when there is a storm:

> . . . makes a tremendous noise like Thunder . . . the Sea rises through the cavity, and covers the ground like snow, for half a mile round it. The cliffs in this part of the coast are dreadful for shipwrecked persons; no escape, whatever, except by chance, the wreckers may be on the watch for plunder and sometimes save a life or two by throwing Ropes down, and drawing the poor creatures up, if they have strength enough to fasten the Ropes round them. *(2nd July 1808)*

Like Sarah Wilmot, Millicent and Lady Wilson visit Stackpole Court, which has clearly been much improved. Millicent finds 'the Gardens, Conservatory, Grape House &c. all in excellent order, and well stocked with fruit. The Dairy is elegantly fitted up with good specimens of old China'. From here they travel to Haverfordwest which, with its narrow streets on a very steep hill, is 'altogether a dangerous place for foot, Horse and Carriage passengers', although the **Castle Inn** is 'a very comfortable house'. She very much admires the church, but rails against the way the fine Gothic pillars have been 'spoilt by their abominable whitewashing'; she finds the castle 'perfect outside, but a miserable building inside, a Gaol'. At **Picton Castle**, where 'there is a good conservatory, orangery, hot house &c.', she sees:

> . . . a Russian horned owl, a female; she lays eggs every year, three of which we saw. She once sat upon Hen's Eggs, hatched three, and attempted to feed the Chickens; she brought them up till they were two months old, and then eats them, not all at once, but a fortnight between each. She has been an inhabitant of the castle eleven years.

There is also a monkey, very savage, has been an inhabitant thirty years. *(7th July 1808)*

Millicent and Lady Wilson next base themselves in Haverfordwest for a few days and take various day trips. They visit **St David's** *(Tyddewi)*, where Millicent admires the cathedral so much that she writes four pages of detailed description in her diary. The town, however, is 'reduced to a few cottages, one wretched inn, which consists of a Kitchen, one (what is called) a parlour, one horrible Bedchamber, and one sitting Room upstairs, whitewashed walls, and broken windows, bad reception for a weary traveller after nineteen dreadful bad rough miles'. Millicent is not an admirer of the Welsh passion for whitewashing, noting that the rage for this 'is so very great, that even the poor trees cannot escape. We saw a Grove today, every one of the trees whitewashed breast high'. The trip to St David's leaves her 'tired to death', but as she has by now been travelling almost non-stop for nearly two months this is hardly surprising.

Next day it is wet and, as Millicent is so exhausted, Lady Wilson goes 'to church by herself, up a very steep Hill, with four Horses and the Coachman, to the great surprise of the Natives'. The following day they arrive in **Fishguard** *(Abergwaun)*, the miserable sea port where Lady Wilson has to send out the coachman and the maid for wine.

Having presumably drunk the wine that was found, they set out next morning for Cardigan, travelling up 'two steeper hills than Lady Wilson ever went up, a tedious and very hot drive, which made us unfit to move for the rest of the day'. They must, however, have had strong constitutions, for the following day they again follow in Sarah Wilmot's footsteps by visiting Cilgerran Castle and the late Sir Benjamin Hammett's grounds. After their river trip they take to their coach again and visit the few remains of the castle at Newcastle Emlyn, the salmon leap at Cenarth, and **St Dogmael's** *(Llandudoch)* Abbey with 'its very small remains, situation bad and Inhabitants the most miserable and wretched we have yet seen, and a shocking bad road to it'.

Despite the general tetchiness and sense of tiredness that is creeping into Millicent's diary, she and Lady Wilson continue to travel on indomitably. They revisit Aberystwyth and Devil's Bridge, which is still 'a compleat Devil's House, and Devil's treatment. Bread musty, and Eggs the same. Took a second view of the fall, which did not appear in such good force as the time before, though there had been a tremendous thunder storm overnight'. Their next and final stopping place on this visit is the small market town of **Llanidloes**, 'a very pleasant town', but the inn does not match the town, for it 'is fit for no one but their own Country People. I believe Lady Wilson was the first with the title of Lady that has ever been in it'.

They are both heartily glad to leave, and they trundle out of Wales and back into England where they arrive home after being away for ten weeks and travelling some 1,676 miles. Yet again, despite grumbles, Millicent and Lady Wilson clearly enjoyed this second visit to Wales for, six years later, the sixty-three year Lady Wilson and her patient companion visit Wales again, although this time for only two weeks out of a second ten-week trip in which they travelled 1,988 miles.

They arrive in **Hay-on-Wye** (*Y Gelli Gandryll*) on the 5th of August, where 'the good ship Wilson, safe in harbour . . . is detained by contrary winds'. However, they manage to leave for **Builth Wells** (*Llanfair-ym-Muallt*) the next day, and for the **Kings Head**, 'the worst Inn in Wales. Bad as it was they fairly turned us out'. Maybe this was not such as disaster after all, as they go to the **Royal Oak** at Rhayader, 'the new Inn which we had been told was much the worst, found it to our great satisfaction much the best and secured a good sleeping room with clean good Beds'. They visit the wells, which then existed in a small wood near the town, where they find:

> . . . three springs all in a triangle, not more than three feet apart, one a strong saline and purgative, another saline and bitter, which is a strong emetic, the third we could not taste, the Pump being broken, suppose it to be like the Bristol Water as the Woman told us it was good for decline. (*8th August 1812*)

During a walk that evening they stop to hear a female Wesleyan preacher who was 'holding forth, her Language was good and impressive, and her voice uncommonly strong, she held out for two hours to a large Congregation, many of them genteel people . . . invited in by a Lady, but as the chapel was small and crowded, we declined the offer'.

They then revisit Brecon, where they go 'from a Pig stye to a new Inn quite a Palace by far the best in Wales'. However they are never still for long, and next day they go on to **Llandovery** (*Llanymddyfri*), stopping to change horses at **Trecastle** (*Trecastell*) where they both walk up a nearby hill and find 'a delightful view . . . quite different scenery from Brecon but equally fine in its way, more wild and mountainous'. Although they do not seem to do any very serious walking on any of their Welsh trips, these two by now quite elderly women must both have been fit.

Having stopped overnight at Llandovery, they visit **Lampeter** (*Llanbedr Pont Steffan*) with Millicent continuing to wax enthusiastic about the scenery which is 'vast and wild'. Once there, her enthusiasm for all that is odd and unusual in churches remains undimmed, for she finds the parish church a 'perfect Barn . . . [with] a curious ancient font stuck in a corner against the wall, square with rich work but much mutilated'. They return to Llandovery for another overnight stop, and then next day retrace their steps to Brecon where they are 'insulted by the waiter as Dinner, altho' ordered the day before by letter was not begun to be prepared when we arrived at half past 4 o'clock the hour it was ordered'. In the evening they stroll, as on their last visit, to the Captain's Walk where they:

... observe a woman milking Ewes in a Hovel. We marched down to her to see the process. Poor creature, she was in a pen with twenty-five Ewes[and]scarce room to stand among them. She milked them from behind and slapped their bags hard to make them give their milk down. Poor thing it was hot and hard work for her; she had to go over them twice. The milk was to be made into Cheese. They are milked for a quarter of a year. *(12th August 1812)*

Having appeared genuinely concerned about this poor woman's labour, Millicent ends with the curious comment that 'it was a very laughable scene'. From Brecon they ride on to Abergavenny, staying at the Angel Inn where they find that, since it is Bonaparte's birthday, the thirty French officers who are imprisoned in the town are having 'a grand Dinner . . . in the room is Bony's Picture, ornamented with a fine wreath of fresh flowers most hastily arranged and at the bottom the Maltese cross which many of them wear'.

They revisit the impressive church and Millicent comments on the wonderful over-life-size wooden figure which, in those days, was thought to be Saint Christopher, but is now known to be part of an enormous medieval Jesse Tree. Hewn from a single piece of oak, it has been described as one of the finest medieval sculptures in the world. Today the oak is revealed in all its original splendour but when Millicent was there it had been 'bedaubed with whitewash'.

Unlike Sarah Wilmot, Millicent does not climb the Skirrid, but comments that from this Holy Mountain even today, 'the Roman Catholics procure the Clay from a Particular spot, keep it in their Houses and when they die put

Llanthony and the Hatterall ridge (Sarah Wilmot, 1802)

some of it in their Coffins, having done this they think they are sure to be saved'. She has little to say about Llanthony other than the fact that it 'is not near so fine as Rievaulx Abbey in Yorkshire'. Arriving safely at Monmouth, Millicent pokes gentle fun at her fascination with old houses, for she sets off 'old House hunting', stopping as always at the odd church en route, this time the old Norman church in Monmouth, with its good 'doorway and arch, font like a thick Punch bowl . . . the rest of the church a perfect Dunghill'.

From Monmouth Millicent and her sometimes testy but indomitable mistress leave Wales for the last time. They stop at **St Briavel's** and, although she is now in England, Millicent's amusing account of the party trying to get breakfast seems to be a good place with which to leave her and her Ladyship. Arriving at the castle, they find that:

> . . . the Gateway is now the **Castle Inn**; alias an Alehouse . . . sent Margaret in as Herald to inquire if we could get breakfast. She being a novice in castle hunting runs out "Oh, my Lady, you cannot possibly get anything here. There is no place to sit down". Seeing a woman approaching hailed her and asked her if there was any other. "Yes, the **George,** much worse than this", but we went in and to Margaret's great surprise found the Room tidy, a fire lighted and the Bed turned into a Bureau. Coachman told us there was not a drop of beer in this famous alehouse. *(21st August 1812)*

And so ends the last Welsh visit of Lady Wilson and her companion, with the lack of wine and uncomfortable inns being just part of a much richer seam of experience, that of exploring great castles, houses and landscape as well as observing the native Welsh. Although Millicent did not see Wales as quite the paradise that other diarists saw, her diaries are still a vivid account of three tours that were greatly enjoyed.

Chapter 4

The Frequent Traveller:
Mary Anne Hibbert (1816, 1823, 1849, 1856, 1858)

*We had intended to go and see some waterfalls, but the morning proved wet . . . the
clouds heeded not our black looks and continued to pour forth their torrents . . . we
had resolved to be wet so set out on foot . . . Robt. Richards led the way and having
found a descent sufficiently precipitous and dirty led us all down into the bed of the
river, where seated on wet rocks, listening to the roar of water and our provisions
moistened by a falling shower we ate our luncheon with considerable zeal. Returned
home wet, dirty and well pleased with our frolick.*   4th October 1816

* * *

Mary Anne Hibbert visited Wales on several occasions during her long life
but her pleasure in her visits was, time and again, overshadowed by
problems. Wet weather frequently dampened both her and her spirits; she
was also dogged by unsuitable beaux, driven by inebriated drivers, or found
no room at the inn. For Mary Anne, stoicism was a very necessary piece of
her travelling hand luggage, and this she seemed to have in plenty, for she
rises above all these minor (and at times major) disasters, and still views all
that she sees in Wales with enthusiasm.

Mary Anne Hibbert (22nd November 1790-1869) was the third of seven
children of William Hibbert of **Hare Hill** in Cheshire. The family also had a
home in Clapham in London, and Mary Anne seems to have spent the latter
part of her life there. The Hibberts were wealthy merchants and Jamaican
planters: Mary Anne's uncle George was famed for both his opposition to the
abolition of the slave trade and his collection of paintings, books and botanical
exotica, whilst her father William appears to have been wealthy enough to be
a gentleman of leisure. In 1784 he married an Elizabeth Greenhalgh. She had
seven children and died, possibly as a result of childbirth, in October 1800.
Two of the children died in infancy; three married, but Mary Anne and her
older sister Sarah remained single. It is clear from the diaries that she kept
throughout her adult life that Mary Anne was both deeply religious and
socially aware. Even today the outcome of her charity can still be seen, as the
almshouses for eight women, erected in 1859 in memory of her father, still
stand in Wandsworth Road in Clapham, London. Mary Anne was an
insatiable traveller throughout her life: she was twenty-six when she first
visited Wales in 1816, and sixty-eight by the time of her final visit in 1858.

The first visit to Wales came about because Mary Anne had received a

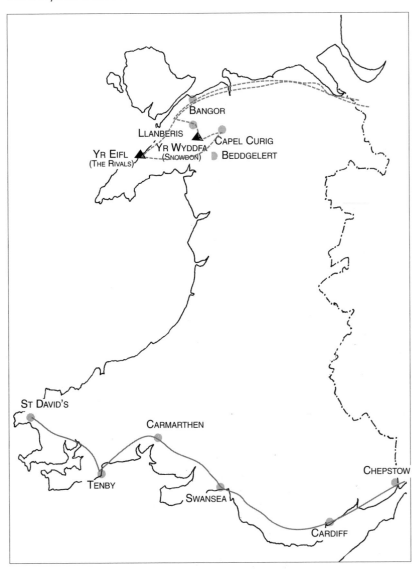

Mary Anne Hibbert.
1816: A visit to friends at Caerynwch with day trips from there (no map).
1823: Wye tour and then to Usk (no map – see Sarah Wilmot 1802 for route).
1849: Journey into north Wales by train.
1856: Train journey to Llandudno, with day trips to places
already illustrated (no map).
1858: A train and coach journey from England to West Wales.

'pressing invitation' to go to **Caerynwch**, near Dolgellau. At the time this fine house was owned by Sir Richard Richards who, a year after Mary Anne's visit became Lord Chief Baron of the Exchequer. She travels into north Wales from Chester, finding that 'the countryside is not particularly interesting excepting as being the entrance to Wales'. At Wrexham it is 'the first day of the races' but she is 'not tempted to join the festive throng' which included 'many nobility and gentry' but she travels on, stopping to see 'the finest view she ever beheld'. She looks down on to a 'most beautiful wooded valley with the Dee winding rapidly beneath, we dismounted and . . . descended the hill on foot, the carriages following where I question whether a carriage had ever gone before but it was well worth a trifling risqué . . . the scene was truly sublime'. So sublime was it that the friend Jane with whom she is travelling is 'seized with such ecstasies at a little rustic bridge and waterfall that I thought she would have fallen into the river'. This is clearly a practice fall for, as the holiday continues, Jane falls regularly into the arms of Robert (one of the sons of Sir Richard), whom she later marries.

As the carriage rumbles on towards **The Hand** at Llangollen, 'a comfortable inn', Mary Anne is enchanted by all she sees – 'mountains, woods, the lovely Dee, an Aqueduct and all the beauties of Nature crowded together'. After a comfortable night, she is ready to go out by seven-thirty but it is, of course, raining so she has to 'growl away the time until after breakfast'. She then follows in the tracks of the curious tourists of the time by visiting Plas Newydd where she 'saw one of the Ladies who popped her head out of the window and answered a question'. From Llangollen the party drives the forty miles to Caerynwch arriving after 8 p.m. to find dinner just over. The house is already very full with a party consisting of Sir Richard Richards and his wife, their daughter Catherine, six of her brothers, and three other guests. Their arrival:

> . . . raised a considerable commotion in the family but they received us very kindly and at our particular request allowed us to go without dinner. We retired to take off our bonnets and smooth our feathers but dressing was out of the question . . . our heads turned round with mountains, waterfalls and so much good company, that after pouring down our throats a comfortable quantity of tea Jane and I retired to our apartment to recover our senses and to rest our bones. (*2nd October 1816*)

But not for long as Mary Anne, in her anxiety to see Cadair Idris, 'slept ill'. At midnight, in bright moonlight, she goes 'to the window and was so much sublimated by what I beheld that I returned to bed still less disposed to sleep. At 6 I again looked forth and was again enchanted'. Breakfast is late – perhaps not surprisingly after a night of sighing over Cadair Idris – and there is yet another visitor, Squire William Griffith Oakeley of Tan y Bwlch, a slate quarry owner. He was clearly aware that his wealth might be an attraction for the ladies, for Mary Anne comments that he presented himself as:

. . . a very great man in his own estimation and certainly a character. Jane and I were advised to set our caps at him but he seemed insensible to our artillery. After breakfast we walked round the grounds, and through a rural little wood to a beautiful waterfall with which we were highly delighted, Jane the more so as we had a little scrambling which afforded her an opportunity of uttering some short and long screams and falling into Robert's arms. *(3rd October 1816)*

Waterfalls and actual falls play no small part in Mary Anne's time in Wales. She and her friends go to **Rhaeadr Ddu** (black falls) where they are 'all enchanted with the scenery . . . Jane escorted by . . . Robert Richards descended to the bed of the river, making a picturesque group for my sketch . . . I afterwards followed her example and lost some of my scrambling fame by falling twice – once into a gentleman's arms'. They carry on to two other falls, a far more:

. . . laborious undertaking as we had to walk above a mile and down some steep precipices . . . it began to rain and we were unable to draw . . . [but] we young people ate our luncheon under a sheltering rock close to the fall. Thus far all was well but a sudden and most unlucky fit of laughing seized Catherine and made her choke till she was quite black in the face and all but gone. A violent blow on the back restored her respiration, but then she almost fainted from the exertion and it cost us some time and more difficulty to get her back . . . the rain from this time descended in torrents. *(3rd October 1816)*

Although the men of the party spend most of their time fox hunting, Mary Anne seems to be a less than enthusiastic rider, and on the one occasion she does go riding her horse is 'seized with a kicking fit. I kept my seat with difficulty but acquired great commendation for my prowess'. Most of her time is passed in a gentle and leisurely fashion with walking, sketching, card games and even, at Barmouth, paddling in the sea which 'was a grand attraction . . . we pursued and overtook the waves and had the pleasure of being wetted by them'. Their journey is every bit as pleasurable and the whole party 'rang the changes upon sublime, magnificent and charming with considerable volubility'.

As well as these gentle pursuits romance is in the air, but all Mary Anne's potential suitors turn out to be unsuitable. They are either, like Squire Oakeley, indifferent to her, or they are overly attentive. On one occasion she is made 'to shake hands . . . with two gentlemen', but she finds their handshakes 'too warm . . . so I gave [them] little encouragement afterwards'. Her other beau is Tom Richards, a clergyman, but he too is rejected because he is 'not very brilliant' and a less than supportive walking companion as she finds to her cost when, on a fine day, accompanied by Jane, Robert and Tom Richards, she sets out to ride and walk up Cadair Idris. They leave the horses some little way from the summit and then scramble to the top. Mary Anne is in heaven, for 'the day was clear and the view of the sea with light clouds floating over it delighted me much . . . the view of the mountains much grander than I expected'. With Mary Anne's bad luck this, of course, does not last and the summit is soon 'enveloped in clouds . . . so we descended a little to a spring to eat our luncheon'. Fortified by lunch, they begin their descent, far more difficult than the ascent:

> . . . Jane went first armed with a pole and Robert. I followed with a pole also and Tom's arm, but this latter support was feeble, and after twice sustaining his faltering steps and twice sharing the disgrace of his falls I begged leave to decline any further obligation, and proceeded as well as I could down the descent and over the slippery stones concealed in heath at the edge of the lake. It was a laborious business but we were proud of our feat and well pleased when we found our horses again . . . it was past 7 and pitch dark when we arrived at Caerynwch. The whole family came out to meet us and received us with three hearty cheers. *(12th October 1816)*

After three weeks in a landscape 'which made Jane scream and me dumb it was so sublime', Mary Anne prepares to leave for home. She gets up on the day of departure feeling 'melancholy' and with 'a heavy heart . . . .it rained terribly, and we were gallantly told Cader was weeping for our departure'. Her melancholy is not perhaps surprising, for Mary Anne had spent an idyllic holiday in a grand house with a wealthy host and in a world in which life was gentle, civil, and hospitable – a paradise indeed.

For some reason there does not appear to be a second visit to the Richards family but seven years later, in July 1823, Mary Anne, now aged thirty-three, sets out on her Welsh travels again. This second visit is to south Wales, with the purpose of taking the Wye tour. Mary Anne travels by carriage with her sisters Sarah and Laetitia, as well as a cousin Henry, who seems to continue Mary Anne's pattern of men who are not much help to her. When they arrive at Ross they all, other than Henry, go out 'to walk & draw . . . Henry is in the dumps & declined drawing saying he was too tired, also much too tired to help Sarah to carry the bread & cheese which we went out with her to purchase for tomorrow's dinner'. As well as the miserable Henry, there are problems at the inn, for the beds are hard and Sarah, who also wrote her diary of the trip, finds that:

> ... [I] did not sleep a wink for fear of not awaking in time, as . . . I knew by the look of the chambermaid that no dependence was to be placed upon her, & so it proved. She never appeared till we were getting into the carriages, & then a little pert "please, miss, to remember the chambermaid" was answered by "I always remember those who do not forget me. You were ordered to call us, & you did not, therefore I give you nothing". The mistress who was standing by said "Quite right, ma'am", so poor Madame Warming pan then went off with her

tail between her legs, & I think the lesson will not be thrown away upon her. *(23rd July 1823)*

Next day 'the morning lowered, & the dripping on the eaves of the houses sounded like the knell of all our hopes', so that by the time they reach Goodrich in their boat, they are 'some of us sufficiently wet & all more than sufficiently cross'. They stop at a ferry house where, in an echo of Sarah Wilmot's 1802 visit, they order:

> . . . a fire, dried ourselves & umbrellas and then drew a table to the window & with admirable philosophy began retouching some of our sketches of yesterday. We were soon rewarded by a gleam of sunshine & in pattens began to scale the heights leading to [Goodrich] Castle . . . our progress was impeded by sundry slight showers but on the whole we fared better than we expected, and after spending about two hours & taking two sketches amongst the ruins, we returned to our boat, ate some bread & cheese & began to think of enjoying ourselves when a storm came aptly enough to remind us of the instability of all human pleasures. *(23rd July 1823)*

Yet despite the feeble Henry and the pouring rain, Mary Anne is clearly an eternal optimist and, when the boat stops by the 'very beautiful' Coldwell Rocks she is easily persuaded to take a five mile walk over the hill, and to meet the boat further downstream. It proves to be an echo of her earlier descent of Cadair Idris. Mary Anne starts off on what proves to be a very slippery path:

> . . . holding the arm of a woman who was our guide. Laetitia followed with a stick to keep her footing, nevertheless she stumbled & fell. I then trusting to my own surefootedness gave her both woman & stick & proceeded alone boldly & fearlessly, but as usual pride had a fall. Not a severe one for the mud was soft, but the liability to such accidents certainly diminished the pleasure of our walk. *(23rd July 1823)*

Poor Mary Anne – a feeble cousin, torrential rain, wet clothes and now a fall – and still 'the rain continues to pour down, to such a degree that we could neither use awning nor umbrellas & the men had hard work to row against it'. As if this were not enough, the scenery also 'altogether disappointed . . . the quantity of wood almost tires the eyes. It wants to be more broken either by rocks or fields or even a variety of green would be a relief'. The last part of the journey was 'a toil of purgatory', and things do not improve when she arrives at Monmouth. It fails to answer her expectations for, although it is a 'handsome well-built town, it is not at all picturesque', and the castle is still 'defiled by pig styes'. Her 'researches in other parts of the town were equally unpropitious but we bought some shoes which the wet weather rendered necessary'. Yet despite all these disappointments, Mary Anne remains curious and cheerful and, with her 'travelling book' to hand, she and Sarah later sally forth to see the 'old church' by the Monnow that Millicent Bant had described some few years earlier. Henry, 'poor fellow, has a bad cold & staid in'.

The tide being unsuitable, they continue their tour on the following day by carriage but, although the weather is now beautiful, their enjoyment of the countryside is marred by the fact that the road is dreadful and it is 'quite impossible to forget how much our necks were in danger but we accomplished it in safety'. At Tintern, like diarists before and after her, she finds that:

> . . . it is impossible to describe the sublimity of the scene! For some time we could not attempt to draw & when we did I was a full half hour in selecting my proportions & was constantly interrupted by the raptures which the different lights streaming through the elegant arches occasioned. We spent easily 4 hours in the abbey & they were hours of unmixed enjoyment chequered only by the reflection that we were so soon to leave it, perhaps for ever. *(24th July 1823)*

Mary Anne's next excitement is to climb to the **Wyndcliff**, a viewpoint high above the river Wye. Her enthusiasm for all she sees is worth quoting in full, for:

> . . . nothing can be more picturesque or beautiful than the path itself, it winds up the rocks in an easy ascent frequently through wood; at

Tintern Abbey (Sarah Wilmot, 1802)

other times you catch glimpses of the lovely view. The path is covered with moss and stones here & there to prevent you slipping. There are seats too at intervals all the way up. The air was heavenly and it was altogether a walk of exquisite enjoyment. Near the top is a very curious cave whether natural or artificial we could not learn, having no guide, but at least it looked like nature. The view from the summit baffles description both in extent and interest. The Severn, the Wye & the union of both with the Bristol Channel, Piercefield and the town & castle of Chepstow are some of the principal objects it embraces. But it was necessary to tear ourselves from this also, though I returned once & again to take a last look. *(24th July 1823)*

From here she rides on to Chepstow, where she determines 'to have no refreshments because it required two things we could not spare, money & time. We went into a pastry cook shop however and ate some currant tarts, traces of which were afterwards very visible on our dress for the juice was abundant'. These female travellers rarely comment on how they pay their way, presumably leaving it to the men of the party but as Mary Anne seems to be the leader of this little party, no doubt because cousin Henry spends a lot of time being 'laid up', she is clearly in charge of the purse. And indeed, a purse it would be for, in the days before a standard banking service, travellers would generally pay their way with coinage, as paper money was not issued (except for a very short period) for less than five pounds, which most inns would have found impossible to change.

So, 'refreshed in body and with minds determined not to be exhausted we proceeded to the castle, a very small part of which is inhabited, the rest is in

Usk Castle (Sarah Wilmot, 1802)

ruins'. But there are more disappointments for the view from the tower is 'spoilt by the state of the tide for the Wye here at low water looks scarcely more than a muddy ditch and the mud banks are frightful. Still the situation of Chepstow must be allowed to be a very fine one'. This second brief visit to Wales is concluded by a visit to both Usk and Raglan, and yet more adventures on the road. As they set out for Usk there is a 'hue & cry' from the post boy, saying that the drag chain on the carriage is broken and he cannot go on in safety. They manage to find a blacksmith who produces a chain which 'whatever might be its defects was not deficient either in length or strength, for it might have been sufficient to drag the wheel of a steam engine. We however accepted it with gratitude'. When they finally arrive in Usk, on 'enquiring for beds we were told they had none. Henry was fairly knocked up and we all stood in need of some repose' but 'after some demur the landlady sent some of her gentleman travellers out of the house & prepared their beds for us'. No doubt the gentlemen were, as was the custom of the time, sent to local homes. Mary Anne wakes next day to another gloomy morning, but she is out by six in order to draw. Even at this early hour, she meets 'several swains of the county [who] accosted us . . . with civility'. From Usk they:

> . . . repaired to Ragland, a very magnificent ruin indeed . . . the ivy is allowed to grow rather too luxuriantly . . . considering it only with a painter's eye the masses of ivy are decidedly too heavy . . . we were plagued by rain . . . which wet our backs and made the grass very damp for our feet. We sighed in vain for a ray of sunshine'. *(25th July 1823)*

This second brief visit must have further whetted Mary Anne's appetite for both north and south Wales for, twenty-six years later in 1849, at the age of fifty-nine, she makes a further visit to north Wales. She travels, this time by train, to **Bangor** with a Charlotte and James Grindlstone. From Bangor she travels by road to Caernarfon, commenting on the Britannia rail bridge which was being built at the time across the Menai Strait , 'the bridge & the monster tunnel as it is called . . . stupendous works both, especially the tunnel through which the railroad is to pass, but it is very far from finished as yet'. In Caernarfon, she stays in 'comfortable' lodgings, rather than an inn. This visit is memorable because she climbs, mostly by pony, two mountains. The first is Snowdon, and her interesting description is worth quoting almost in its entirety. With her travelling companions she takes the Llanberis path, which is the longest and easiest of the several routes up Snowdon. She and her party begin, as did most tourists of the time, by hiring ponies and guides from the **Royal Victoria Hotel** at **Llanberis**, and then riding:

> . . . to within half a mile of the summit which was reached soon after 1 o'clock . . . the whole under a cloud. As there was nothing to be seen we determined, after bespeaking the room [in the hut on the mountain] for the night, to eat our dinner . . . towards 3 o'clock the

mist rolled off & we had the most beautiful effects possible, the landscape appearing at intervals between wreaths of mist. Soon it was clear on all sides & after enjoying the panorama from the summit we walked . . . as far as the saddle where there is a magnificent view . . . a very glorious one it was, the sun going down behind the sea, which seemed like liquid gold . . . we had tea as soon as it was dark & then came the night which was misty & windy so that we saw little of the moon or anything else. I tried to lie down on one of the beds, but bad smells & other disagreeables made me soon quit that locality & I got some sleep, as did my companions also, by the fireside. We wrote letters at intervals. I was struck with one of the guides when he brought up hot water, coals etc. for the night asking if we should like a Testament. They seem a very religious people. Morn came at last but brought disappointment, for the mist was so thick that we could see nothing, & the wind so high it was scarcely possible to stand out of doors, added to which I felt far from well. However just at sunrise there was a break & we had several vistas of a golden sky & beautiful country . . . once more the clouds closed densely round us, & we resigned ourselves to our fate, & bent all our energies to boiling our kettle for breakfast when we finished all our provisions satisfactorily. The guide . . . though he bought a pony told me he did not think I could sit it [as] . . . the wind was so high. We set out therefore on foot, I helped by the guide . . . then it was discovered that before I had mounted the pony one of the bags had been lost. We were then past all the great difficulties so the guide thought we might do without him & he went back for our missing treasure which however I had little hope could have escaped being blown away in such a tornado. We struggled on . . . [once] home, I saw a Doctor who advised me to go immediately to bed. *(25th September 1849)*

The climb clearly exhausts her, for she spends several days feeling unwell and having disturbed nights. Eventually she is sufficiently recovered to do further explorations, although they are often on 'a dripping morning'. She goes to **Llyn Cwellyn**, which is 'fringed by a very striking mountain' and on, via **Beddgelert**, to **Pont Aberglaslyn**, 'a very beautiful walk & the situation of the bridge quite as striking as I expected . . . passed through **Nant Gwynant** valley a more magnificent scene . . . the summit of Snowdon invisible the whole day . . . but the mist gave a mysterious grandeur to the scene which we thought compensated'. Her next adventure is to be 'up with the lark' to see the **Nant Ffrancon** valley and **Llyn Idwal**. At Nant Ffrancon she sees 'a most sublime effect of clouds which heightened inexpressibly the grand scenery through which we passed'; whilst Llyn Idwal is 'a sort of mountain tarn surrounded by steep rocks with one deep fissure which is called the Devil's Kitchen'. It was here that Charles Darwin had originally failed to realise that this was a glacial landscape: a mistake he corrected in his later writings.

Once she had recovered from her Snowdon expedition, Mary Anne does a second gentler mountain ascent, this time to **The Rivals** (*Yr Eifl*) on the Llyn Peninsula, and for which her notes are far briefer than for her Snowdon climb. This second adventure starts off on 'a fine morning . . . took a pony to carry me up the hills but as it happened I used it very little for the road was too rough to trust to anything but my legs. Had our luncheon at the hut; splendid views a very enjoyable day. A hail storm with thunder & lightening as we returned but we did not get much wet'. And so ends Mary Anne's second visit to the grandeur of north Wales where, despite the persistent rain, her enthusiasm for the mountains and the landscape is as fresh as on her earlier visit.

In 1856, by which time Mary Anne is sixty-six, she and her other unmarried sister Sarah, make a final visit to north Wales, travelling by train to **Llandudno**, which was fast becoming a fashionable resort. Her diary for this visit is a brief one, but her comments still give a flavour of holiday life for the genteel tourist of the time. When they arrive at the **Queens Hotel** they have their usual lack of luck for they find 'nothing had been done for us . . . and after getting some indifferent refreshments', they have to set out to find lodgings for themselves. Unlike her earlier energetic visit, with its two mountain ascents, this visit is a gentle one, and the days roll by, suitably perhaps for her age and gravitas, with much socialising with other visitors to the town whom she appears to have known beforehand, sketching, and of course, rain. On one particularly stormy night, she comments that her 'landlord [who] had been out in the storm, came to my room by mistake which was rather alarming but I took it quietly'.

She does, however, do a little exploring. She visits Conwy Castle where she sketches on a day when, although there was 'rain as we returned home . . . on the whole our day was a fortunate one'. On another occasion she goes over the Menai Bridge to Beaumaris on a day that 'turned out beautiful & we greatly enjoyed our drive. The Menai Strait offers many enchanting views . . . alighted at Glengarth [**Glyngarth**] . . . the lady was from home but they gave us leave to walk on the terrace & very charming it was [with a view of] Snowdon . . . with a night-cap on'. She and her party dine at Beaumaris, but had to wait for a 'convocation of clergy to be fed first about 60 in number . . . dined indifferently on the relics of the feast for which we paid as if it had been first-hand'. This is another good day for 'we, weather, trains & all prospered – we reached home about 8 & found a fire had been successfully lighted in our smoking chimney which I hailed with pleasure & to crown our good luck a heavy shower fell soon after we got in'. Another visit is by carriage to **Gloddaeth**, where Mary Anne finds 'an old house built in the reign of Elizabeth & very curious especially the Hall. The rooms were undergoing painting but I should like to see it when finished. I believe the grounds are beautiful'.

From Llandudno, Mary Anne travels on to Capel Curig to more lodgings, and where rain makes their few days there a literal as well as a metaphorical wash-out. She then goes to the Royal Victoria hotel in Llanberis, from where she had so gallantly begun her ascent of Snowdon some seven years earlier. She finds there are 'coals that did not burn, food we did not know how to eat, table linen in most disgraceful rags & attendance very remiss. We certainly cannot recommend it to any one & beautiful as the scenery is I am glad to go'. While she is there she goes to church and comments that there are 'two clergymen but no gown & only one surplice between them which was doffed & donned in public'- a brief glimpse of the poverty that would have been the lot of many Welsh clergy at that time. Her health is clearly beginning to be a problem as she is 'troubled with a derangement in my interior' and the Mary Anne of this visit is a sad contrast to the lively young woman who enjoyed such a carefree visit to Caerynwch some forty years earlier. Yet, despite the fact that rain often meant that she could not get out to explore, she still feels her visit was 'a fortunate one'.

So fortunate indeed, that she returns to Wales again in 1858, this time to south and west Wales, travelling by train as far as Tenby with her sister Sarah and Supemis, their maid. As on previous holidays, minor misfortunes dog her, yet she remains undaunted by them. The letter written asking for a carriage from the train to Tenby had not arrived and in consequence they can only get one that is too small for their luggage. When they finally arrive in Tenby, the letter sent ahead seeking lodgings had also arrived too late and so they have to stay overnight at the **Coburg Hotel**. Next day they do find suitable lodgings and from there Mary Anne makes various sorties into the surrounding countryside, including a visit to Manorbier, where she inspects 'the inside of the ruin in which we found considerable interest . . . [it] is kept locked up as all ruins must be in this country or they would soon be destroyed. It is a great place for Pic Nics.' She reacts to Pembroke in much the same way as had Millicent Bant, over forty years earlier, for she finds it 'has little to recommend it, a long straggling street & we saw no good houses. The castle in a sad ruinous state but picturesque, the round tower which they call the keep is still roofed'.

At Tenby itself, although some of her time is spent feeling unwell, she and Sarah both enjoy bathing, walks and drives along the beach. They also, being genteel and devout, go 'to a meeting of the Church Missionary Society . . . a missionary in India & China made a very interesting speech, but the proceedings were rather long & we were not home till near 10'. She is often forced to stay inside because of the rain, writing letters and finding herself 'badly off for a book'. She sees a rainbow, and also has 'a capital view of the comet': this would have been Donati's comet, which he first observed and recorded in 1858; it was visible for several months that year and it clearly fascinates Mary Anne, as her sighting (or non-sighting of it) is a recurrent theme in her diary. From Tenby she goes on to St David's, where she faces more problems. She arrives after a hot and tiring journey and greets her potential landlord with:

... 'you expected us of course'. He looked aghast & said "why the ladies we expected arrived ½ an hour ago". Here was a catastrophe. The first comers had actually been installed into our rooms & what was more refused to give them up. The landlord threw himself upon our mercy having been out talked by the other party & for the sake of peace we gave in & slept in the most miserable dog hole I have ever occupied. Truth to say I was somewhat cross. I was not able to take out anything having no room & spent the evening dozing & abusing the so called ladies . . . the people excused themselves by saying it was rarely ladies ever came here & two parties in one day was a thing unheard of. *(17th September 1858)*

Next day Mary Anne's maid, Supemis, has much the same task as Lady Wilson's coachman many years previously, that of exploring places on the mistress's behalf and reporting back. She is sent, on a beautiful morning, to explore St David's Head and returns looking:

... so hot & tired . . . I was glad I had not attempted it though she said it was well worth the exertion. On our return we met the ladies & they grinned at us most maliciously. We found however that they meant to decamp today so we may stay . . . [although] the food here is not tempting & requires all the help of their fine air to get it down . . . Welsh is much spoken in St. David's. Our guide today scarcely understood a word of English, so that it would not be possible to learn much from him. *(18th September 1858)*

Mary Anne clearly finds St David's very interesting. She writes a good deal about her explorations in the cathedral, which she finds is 'an immense pile of a building but great part is in ruins & what is still used sadly wants renovation. The carving of the roof is very fine, so is the Bishops throne. The arches are generally Saxon but some Gothic, not highly ornamented'. The Bishop's Palace also meets with her cautious approval for it 'has been in its way the handsomer building of the two but . . . is quite a ruin & as it is not locked up from the public of course if gets rapidly worse'. Mary Anne is also much struck with the 'observance of the Sabbath, noting that 'our landlady went to the early service, then attended the school & in the evening went to some place of worship again though she has a baby & her house to attend to'.

After three days in St David's Mary Anne goes by train from Haverfordwest to Chepstow, a much speedier way of travelling than in the slow horse-drawn carriages she would have taken when she began her travels to Wales so many years earlier. Although she thinks she will 'like the place well enough' she finds that dinner at the Beaufort hotel is:

... nothing to boast of. A brace of pheasant, one of which was old & of the other half the flesh has been shot away, some good salmon, pudding forgotten. Beds not feeling very fresh, all soft & touzled I had not a good night. A good deal of rain fell & we hear the railway more than is pleasant. *(21st September 1858)*

She wakes up to rain, as she has so often on her Welsh travels and finds, to her horror, that the 'enemies of St. David's have pursued us here. Supemis met their maid on the stairs & instead of fighting each other each party began laughing', which seems to imply that, in the end, humour rather than rancour prevailed. At last the rain stops and she is able to venture out to:

> ... the castle which is prepared for a flower show ... there was nothing much to see excepting some cut flowers. The dahlias, asters & holly hocks were very handsome, there was also a good show of fruit especially pears & apples. The thing was badly managed, for they did not open as soon as they had promised & we were kept standing a weary long time on the damp grass. I did not see much smart company or any indeed. A beautiful rainbow. *(22nd September 1858)*

After a few more days spent visiting acquaintances, having indifferent meals and going to church Mary Anne, like so many earlier tourists, visits Piercefield and is actually shown over the house 'which is handsomely furnished & some very fine old chimney pieces'. She revisits Tintern, even though she had thought her previous visit would be her last, and finds that it looks 'as beautiful as ever ... the old man who shews it is a curiosity ... & has been there above 30 years making a very good thing of it'. She continues to comment on the comet, sometimes finding that cloud obscures it but on one wonderful occasion, finding it the 'more brilliant [and] I think the finest I have ever seen'. And so, with this brilliant view of the comet, Mary Anne says 'farewell' to Wales for the last time. Although she sketches and sketches on all her trips, the sadness is that, however indifferent they might have been, they have disappeared, like the comet, for ever from sight.

Over the next few years, Mary Anne, despite increasingly frail health, continues to travel, but only in England. Finally ill-health does put an end to her travels and in 1866, three years before her death, her diary comments more and more on her health problems. Her last entry, on 31 August is very sad, for she says that on this day, 'I think I saw no-one else. Suffered a good deal from heat but it cooled towards the end of the time & I was better but obliged to have someone to sit up with me'.

Mary Anne Hibbert may not have had success with gentleman, and may have ended her life without close family around her, but her diaries of her travels to Wales remain as an account of a life which, genteel though it was, included many adventures, not least of which would have been climbing two mountains, in cumbersome and heavy clothing, at the age of fifty-nine.

Chapter 5

The Picturesque Traveller:
Margaret Martineau's journey from St Albans
into north and south Wales (1824)

*To ride upon level ground along the most beautiful scenery . . . without a rut or an
inequality of ground and with a neat parapet wall Simplon fashion so as to do away
with all fears of a roll down the precipice which giddy heads will sometimes have.
Nothing could be more beautiful than the ride today and our postillions seemed by
their slow pace to be aware that we were picturesque tourists . . . and that we did
[not] want to rattle through all that was fine.*

Margaret Martineau on the 'great Holyhead road', 27th June 1824

* * *

Margaret Martineau (1798–1891) was a lucky as well as a picturesque
traveller for, by the time she travelled to Wales, tourism was well in its stride
and both roads and inns were improving. Nevertheless, Wales was still not
for the faint-hearted; for when Margaret holidayed there in 1824 with her
uncle David and five cousins, there was rain and more rain (shades of Mary
Anne Hibbert) as well as occasional problems with horses and those inns that
had not yet seen fit to respond to the ever increasing numbers of 'picturesque
tourists'.

Margaret was a cousin of two distinguished people, both of whom were
deeply committed to the Unitarian faith: Harriet Martineau, passionate
advocate for the abolition of slavery, political economist and an early
sociologist, and her brother James, one of the most influential theologians
and philosophers of his time. Margaret too was deeply committed to the
Unitarian faith and to its three tenets: freedom, reason and tolerance. The
Huguenot, Unitarian Martineaus were descended from a Gaston Martineau
who left France in 1686. Margaret's father, Peter Finch Martineau, began his
working life as a dyer in Norwich; then became a sugar-refiner before joining
a firm of bankers. Margaret, an accomplished artist, was the youngest
daughter of his second marriage. In 1829 she married a Samuel Francis
Thomas Wild and the couple, who seemed to have had a happy marriage,
had six children to whom Margaret was an affectionate mother. Margaret
was ninety-three when she died in 1891, and her obituary described her as an
'esteemed and venerable lady', who in her 'long and exemplary life has done
much in an unostentatious way to make her beloved by all who knew her'.

Margaret was definitely an intrepid traveller, and always able to find the

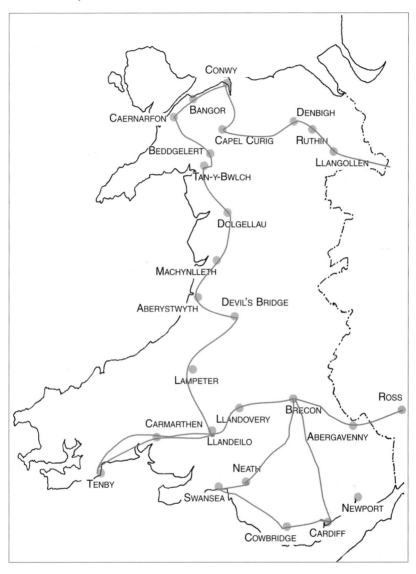

Margaret Martineau.
1824: An extensive journey throughout Wales.

silver lining, whatever the cloud. She inevitably goes to many of the same places as the earlier diarists, but her lively descriptions of all she sees add another dimension to life and travel in Wales in the first quarter of the nineteenth century. Her month-long journey of 998 miles covers both north and south Wales, and begins in Llangollen which she clearly loves, for she 'never knew a place that grew upon one's affections as it does'. From her 'clean and homeish inn' she does two walks. The first is a gentle one to see:

> . . . [the] residence of the venerable blues, a little close pent up cottage with the fine vale carefully shut out. We were fortunate enough to catch a glimpse of the ladies now rather advanced in years; their grey hair hanging from beneath their Welch hats and habits made one doubt their sex, but at all events stamped them as oddities . . . we afterwards walked again thro' the ladies grounds and had an excellent view and a bow from the oddities as they were walking uncovered in the front of their cottage, their grey powdered locks hanging down their backs. One of them had a red ribbon slung across her which we were told was an order presented by some foreign prince. *(25th June 1824)*

The second is rather more strenuous. She walks first to the ruined Cistercian abbey of **Valle Crucis**. It is a beautiful walk 'every turn giving you a view of the mountains in a different position; the ruin itself is fine standing in a field shaded by light and elegant ash trees, part . . . now converted into a farm house, where we had some excellent milk'. Their little guides who, 'by the bye were rather beggars, each of them petitioning for a new gown', give her a Welsh lesson. Next she does 'a rather fatiguing walk' by climbing the hill fort of **Dinas Brân**, with its ruined medieval castle on its summit. She and her cousins are again petitioned by 'numerous children [who] offered themselves as our guides each anxious to secure a parasol or sketchbook as a certificate of her official capacity. A woman at the top provided us with some excellent milk'.

Margaret is something of a whirlwind traveller, rarely spending more than a few hours in any one place, and from climbing Dinas Brân she dashes on to Denbigh where, although the inn seems dirty, she nevertheless has a 'most merry dinner, the excellent ale inspired us and everything looked really cleaner than we expected'. They all walk 'to the remains of the castle . . . our guide could hardly speak English. There was a lime kiln smoking most furiously, my uncle [asked] whether it always smoked in that way. The man with the utmost simplicity said "No, sir, it sometimes smokes the other"'.

As Margaret ventures further into north Wales along the Vale of Llangollen she passes 'over a deep, wild & richly wooded chasm along the bed of which a considerable torrent foamed from rock to rock. It was really grand, the most decidedly mountain scene we had yet met with'. She stops to admire the famous **Swallow Falls** near **Betws-y-Coed**, 'a very fine and romantic scene, well clothed with beautiful trees hanging from every cleft of the rock'. At Capel Curig she finds another 'clean and comfortable' inn, but 'a drizzling rain prevented our taking advantage of the fine scenery around us'. However, it clears up next day, and they all decide to go to Bangor for the day. She is in ecstasies as she travels through Nant Ffrancon, for 'the mountains were now more rugged than ever, the clouds were just rolling over their heads and a grander scene can hardly be imagined . . . the river rushing over the rocks and the barren sides of the mountains more broken and more rugged than any British scene I had yet beheld'. As she draws near to Bangor there is a sudden change of scene with 'a rich woody valley stretching down to the sea . . . the sea is always interesting and beautiful and I felt that I should sooner get tired of the grand, nay awful view we had left than I should the calm and peaceful one we were enjoying'.

Even this paradise has its sadness for as they journey to Bangor 'the fall of one of our horses rather distressed us, but the poor thing was soon raised again and except [for] a little trembling carried us as well as if nothing had happened, though a more complete fall I never saw'. Back at Capel Curig she climbs up a hill at the back of the inn to a cottage where a 'clean nice woman' gives her some milk and she watches the woman's mother 'spinning the yarn for worsted stockings. They amused us by examining our dresses. They could not speak English, so we could have little communication with them but by means of kindly signs and friendly smiles, a language always understandable'.

Rain again interferes with Margaret's travel plans but she amuses herself at the inn with 'drawing, mending gloves . . . roaming over the house and congratulating ourselves on being obliged to travel. Dined early. Eliza, always unfortunate, found some flies between the crusts of her gooseberry pie where yesterday she found some mould'. There is rain and more rain but Margaret remains philosophical, arguing that at least it keeps her free from dust, but also musing on whether 'those I am travelling with have shadows or whether like Peter Schlemiel [author of *The Man Who Sold His Shadow*] they have sold them. I am in some doubt as to my own. I have scarcely seen it since I left St Albans'. Margaret wakes up again next day to more rain but the gallant party drives to Llanrwst where Lord Gwydir, who:

> . . . has a shabby old thing, **Gwydir Castle**, adjoining the town . . . with his lady was expected today . . . the good people were all on the watch and when our carriage drove up they flocked round us fully expecting to see my lady and set the church bells ringing (a fine peal of two). We however told them that they were not up when we left Capel Curig, and we saw a procession of tenantry set off to meet them and draw them in. *(30th June 1824)*

From here Margaret and her cousins set out for Conwy where she dismisses the castle as 'fine but it is such a hackneyed subject that it did not strike one as new'. She finds the **White Lion** at Conwy 'tho small and dark is really not at all uncomfortable . . . surprising! a beautiful morning and we made the most of it'. Making the most of it meant doing a little light trespassing as she goes to see **Benarth Hall,** a private house on the banks of the river, despite:

Gwydir Castle

... being warned in English and Welch that we should be prosecuted as we passed through; on our return a gentleman followed us. We hurried on expecting a reprimand but not so, with the greatest politeness he opened the gate and begged we would walk over the grounds either then or in the afternoon ... we thanked [him] but told him we were then leaving Conwy. I hoped we thanked him properly but his politeness took us so completely by surprise that I feel that I at least did not. *(1st July 1824)*

From Conwy, Margaret and her cousins go to Bangor again, riding over Penmaenmawr, which she finds very safe though comments that the road is still 'very narrow with a mountain almost perpendicular, the sea dashing against the base'. They settle in to the 'superb' **Penrhyn Arms**, and then walk to see the all but completed Menai suspension bridge, but:

... hunger impelled four of us into a bakers in search of luncheon ... and by some means or other we missed the other three; so Eliza, Sarah, Lucy and self walked on in the rain ... the rain increased but we had each an umbrella ... when we reached the **Ferry House** we were quite wet, so we went boldly in, asked for a sitting room, called for some ale and then begged admittance to the kitchen to dry ourselves by a roaring fire we saw there. We drank our ale, walked down the garden to the ferry to see the wonderful and beautiful building now nearly ready for centre chains . . . [then] set off in a still heavier rain for our walk back, quite pleased with having seen the bridge and quite amused with our adventure. *(1st July 1824)*

Margaret is not quite such an enthusiast for mountains as many of these early travellers, for she writes 'I do not know why . . . but I feel no wish to return to them . . . I feel not the least attachment to the place'. She wonders whether it is because 'the mountains are too distant to inspire one with awe and the country not cultivated enough to make one love it, or it may merely be that it rained all the time we were there'. Day after day of rain can dampen the spirits of even the most enthusiastic of travellers, but when Margaret awakes next day to yet another 'wet morning [with] a settled drizzling rain' she sees, as always, the silver lining, reflecting that she is 'at least part of a large happy party in a large house'. Margaret and her cousins go next to Caernarfon where the castle and the quay are 'fine' but the town 'dirty'. Next day it is *still* raining but at breakfast she finds that suddenly luck is with her for while she is paying her:

> . . . respects to the toast and eggs, the sun almost burst forth, so we set off . . . prepared for a good jolting . . . we unfortunately laughed at first setting off and the jolting quite prevented us stopping the laugh the whole way. We saw nothing of the mountains till we came just over the lakes then they burst upon us in the grandest way. The lakes spread below us, with the mountains rising abruptly behind and around them . . . [we] left our jolting vehicles and more jolting roads for two two-oared boats . . . and had a most soothing row after the rough ride. The clouds rolling about upon the mountains increased perhaps their grandeur though we would fain have had some sunshine. *(3rd July 1824)*

Despite having had such a jolting start to the day the intrepid Margaret and her cousins do a four mile walk in the Llanberis pass. First they stop 'at the public house at the entrance of it, got some bad biscuits and some worse ale'. They then set off in 'hard rain . . . we thought it would only be a shower but the rain persisted heavily and steadily during our four miles'. They were all obliged 'to jump from one [stone] to another to avoid being over our shoes in water. The scenery was however quite grand enough to make amends for wet shoes and tired legs, though . . . a mountain pass did not appear to advantage through a thick umbrella'. Throughout her diary Margaret's happy disposition shines out and she regards this as a most delightful day and one that she will never forget for 'it is astonishing how soon the minor evils of travelling, such as wet feet [and] pouring rain slip from one's memory and leave nothing but the lasting and vivid impression of the rich and grand mountains, the smooth and tranquil lakes'. Added to which is the pleasure of a day spent 'with those who enjoy it and are disposed to make the best of every enjoyment and the lightest of every little grievance'.

The following morning is a Sunday and Margaret who is 'up betimes' has gone out to sketch when:

> . . . four different people took me to task for drawing on a Sunday. They did it very respectfully and I was pleased with their scrupulousness. I found I was on the road to a church to which they were flocking. By its being so early in the day I should think that they were Methodists . . . they were serious and well-meaning and that I might not shock their feelings any more, after explaining that I had stolen the hour from sleep, that I was a traveller and that I was going to church after breakfast, I moved into a little by-lane to finish my drawing. *(4th July 1824)*

Margaret next travels to Beddgelert, still describing the scenery in glowing terms and sketching furiously wherever she goes. In the glow of a wonderful sunset at Pont Aberglaslyn her cousin 'Lucy stopped to sketch and had a crowd of 19 round her to see her and to say "Dim Sasenag (no English)" to all her questions'. More journeying on, this time along the Nant Gwynant pass, 'as beautiful a pass as we have yet seen not even excepting Llanberis. It is richer and not so desolate as that is'. On a ten-mile walk later in the day she sees the summit of Snowdon for the first time. Usually shrouded in mist, it was, she says 'the first [time] he had taken his nightcap off in our presence . . . the scene was, not to use too strong an expression, enchanting and the innumerable little streams dashing from rock to rock added much to the delight of both sound and sight'.

The following day, she leaves 'sweet beautiful grand Beddgelert full of regrets at being obliged to part from it so soon . . . Mrs Pritchard (mine hostess) Kitty, the waiter and all the household assembled at the leave taking'. Clearly too much sublime scenery can blunt the senses for gentler views, for Margaret finds, as she travels on to Tan y Bwlch, that a 'few days ago we should have called it fine the whole way but yesterday's walk has made us wonderfully fastidious and we found fault with the salt marshes, tho' flanked by high mountains on three sides and open to the sea on the other'. However, she soon discovers that:

> . . . [the] marshes we had been abusing were part of the redeemed land. At present they do not promise to reward the labour that has been bestowed on them and unless some part of [the] estate produce more than they do, Mr Madocks's ingenuity and perseverance will have been expended on a bad soil. The embankment will be a constant expense to keep in order. *(6th July 1824)*

This was the embankment built in 1800 by the rich and philanthropic William Madocks who reclaimed the marshland in order to build the new town of **Tremadoc** (*Tremadog*). He was bankrupted by its construction, but the thriving port of **Portmadoc** (*Porthmadog*) grew up because of it, greatly helped by the then booming slate industry. The embankment today still stands with both a road and the famous Ffestiniog steam railway running along its top.

When Margaret attempts to go to Rhaeadr Ddu, where Mary Anne Hibbert had done her falling into gentlemen's arms, she finds neither gentlemen's arms nor waterfall. Their non-English-speaking guide soon gets them all up to the top of their shoes in mud, and Margaret beats a retreat, leaving the others 'struggling with the mud and jumping with the agility of goats from one stepping stone to another, nine times out of ten missing them and coming . . . plump in the mud . . . [and] getting prettily bespattered'. However she has problems of her own when she gets back to the inn for she finds that the carriage, for which her uncle has the key, is locked, and in it is her half finished letter and work box, so that she is without 'one resource but the writing of this tremendously long account of the transaction of the day'.

Undeterred by their wet walk in the Llanberis pass, Margaret and her cousins set out doggedly in more rain the next day for a walk to the **Cynfal Falls** where there is nearly a serious accident. The rain is getting harder and harder, and she finds that:

> . . . the descent to the falls is difficult, at least slippery . . . we were clambering down to the principal fall and our numerous party was scattered amongst the brakes and young trees that clothe its sides, when suddenly I saw one of the foremost slip down the smooth side of what appeared to be an almost perpendicular rock. She went so gently that I thought it was intentional, till I observed that she was sitting. I then found that it was indeed a slip. She stopped and we all exclaimed 'she is safe', when again she slid on and we lost sight of her. It was a dreadful moment. We all fancied her fallen into the torrent and dashed to pieces against the rocks . . . our anxiety then was to get her safely up. We females were all in too great a tremor to attempt then what in our firmest moments we could not have done . . . my uncle found his way down and clinging to a tree with one hand, with the other and with the little guide's assistance, she was rescued from her perilous situation, for all the time she was clinging to nothing but grass . . . a bruised ankle, a torn stocking and a few bruises were all the damage. We cannot any of us give much account of the waterfall. *(7th July 1824)*

But their troubles are not yet over, for the bedraggled little party still has to struggle back to the inn in the driving rain. So soaked are they that when they arrive they have to undress almost completely to allow the landlady to dry their clothes. They are all 'glad to take refuge in not very clean beds . . . without sheets and with fleas, four of us in one bed, but we were very merry . . . when our things were dry our kind hostess insisted on our taking a glass of wine and some biscuits'. Even though the Welsh were becoming more accustomed to tourists, generous Welsh hospitality, it seems, remains unabated.

Margaret and her party definitely have good constitutions for the rigours of tourism. After this adventure they drive back to Tan y Bwlch for dinner, then set out for Dolgellau, an eighteen-mile journey over a dreadful road that takes them five and a quarter hours. There fortune smiles on them as they find the 'accommodations excellent and the people extremely civil'. Despite this long and arduous day, Margaret and her cousins set out on a day trip to 'the singular looking town of Barmouth', where the inn is still 'dirty and uncomfortable'. The following day there 'is a long and rough stage for the poor horses' to Machynlleth where they get a 'cold dinner' and where they regretfully say goodbye to north Wales, with its 'pointed mountains and rapid torrents', exchanging it for countryside with 'round topped hills and quiet streams, a bad exchange unless fine weather be thrown into the balance'.

Margaret's south Wales journey begins at Aberystwyth which she finds 'extremely neat, the lodging houses on the beach delightful, and the air the purest possible . . . we passed a delightful day doing nothing but watching the waves . . . employment enough for one day for me at any time. I am sure I am the idlest of mortals'. Whilst there they enquire about the curious phenomenon of the Jumpers, an aspect of Welsh non-conformity, when charismatic preachers used the 'hwyl', a high-pitched, sing-song delivery, to so affect their congregations that they did indeed jump; jumping that was probably a mixture of the spiritual and the sensual and which sometimes went on for hours. 'Jumping' was such an unusual and curious thing that it became something of a tourist attraction in its own right. However:

> . . . we found that they had left off jumping. We did not feel any inclination to go and hear most probably a long service in a language we did not understand, unless it stood some chance of seeing the extraordinary inspiration of jumping, which ceremony took place I believe in the middle of the service. I should have been half afraid of going lest I should have been entrapped. Also we must all have felt how catching laughing and hysterics are, why may not jumping be as infectious. I shall also have been afraid of laughing had I gone, and however ridiculous any particular tenets may appear, the professors of them are in earnest and are really sincere. We ought to look carefully to ourselves before we venture to ridicule our neighbour. To me in particular as a Unitarian the slightest shadow of illiberality is unpardonable. There's a sermon I declare. *(11th July 1824)*

From Aberystwyth they follow the usual tourist trail to the falls at Devil's Bridge. The inn had been renovated since Millicent and Lady Wilson grumbled so much about it, for Margaret is 'in comfortable quarters although 'mine hostess [is] civil to us but snappish and grumpy to everyone round her'. The falls, a 'roaring, boiling, angry torrent called for my attention in a tone too loud to be unnoticed' and, despite their fright at Cynfal, they decide, with a guide, to descend the steep path to see them from below the bridge.

Devil's Bridge (Drawing by David Cox, c. 1820)

Margaret is clearly very frightened at the prospect, 'for the descent appeared tremendous; [the guide] took us each separately and when it came to my turn I felt that I would more gladly have seated myself in a dentist's horrific chair'. However, she does go and recovers her composure sufficiently to pen a very interesting account of what she sees:

> . . . the scene from below is extremely grand, the river, pent into chasms in many places not, I should think, more than three feet across, foams and roars amongst the rocks, sometimes forming a passage under them, then appearing one sheet of white froth, then dashing down the rock, then for a few yards appearing quite exhausted by its own rage, passing quietly along. It was a grand scene, but it almost took away my breath and it was a great effort to raise my hand to wave to my uncle who was standing on the bridge just over us. *(11th July 1824)*

Back at the inn there is a different kind of roaring. They are having tea when:

> . . . the most violent and horrible screams and groans and swearing assailed our ears. We went to the window and, finding the uproar came from the room below us, we locked the door then returned to listen. The noise increased and soon a poor unhappy man was dragged out by five other men. He appeared in the most dreadful state of derangement, struggled to get free and begged to die on the spot. At one time I

thought they would all have been over the precipice. The greatest horror seized us all of fancying it was our guide, and that he might have [been] taken in this way whilst with us. As soon however as he was quite gone and all was quiet we unlocked the door and rang for the waiter. He appeared with a face as white as our own, but satisfied us instantly by telling us it was a man in the neighbourhood who was tipsy. A glass or two reduces him to the state of derangement that we had witnessed. A prospect of unpleasant dreams for me tonight, being pushed down a precipice by the drunken man. *(11th July 1824)*

Next day, having recovered both from the roaring of waterfalls and the local drunk, the party travel on to nearby Hafod, but by the time of Margaret's visit there is 'no owner to enjoy it . . . the estate being in the Chancellor's hands just now'. She is, however, able to walk in the grounds, viewing all she sees with a picturesque eye for 'the path was just in comfortable order, neither rough, steep, nor trim, but just as it ought to be amidst such scenery, wild and natural, all the better I dare say for being a little out of order'.

There is little respite to the continual travelling and, after a second night in the Hafod Hotel, Margaret goes first to **Tregaron** for breakfast on 'a bad road and not a good inn when we got there, yet we managed to make a good breakfast in spite of nasturtium coffee'; then on to Lampeter where she is interested in:

> . . . a large college that was being built for 60 young men for the Welsh churches. Our clergyman acquiring a grammatical knowledge of the language but finding it almost impossible to acquire a true pronunciation, the generality of the people have become Methodists. So the Bishop of St David's has founded this college to reclaim the strayed sheep by giving them pastors whom they can understand. *(13th July 1824)*

This is a reference to the fact that many clergy in Wales were English and had little understanding of either the language or the culture of the country in which they were obliged to minister. It was hoped that this new college, one of the oldest in Britain, would provide Welshmen intent on entering the Anglican ministry in Wales with 'an opportunity of securing a sound and liberal education', a necessary attribute for such a career.

From Lampeter, Margaret plans to travel on to Carmarthen but there is a problem. Where are the horses? Eventually they appear having come straight from ploughing. The first of the post boys mounts 'steadily and properly' for he and his horse clearly know each other well but a real fiasco occurs with the second:

> . . . a boy weighing 20 stone and aged 50 put his foot in the stirrup and tried to spring, but alas the saddle, not made to fit very exactly refuses to bear his prodigious weight and round it came. The man looked

dismayed and the fellow horse gave a sympathetic rear, but as there was someone at the head of each horse, holding it as if a whole regiment of soldiers were firing around us, no accident ensued. The mistress advised John's having a chair to mount by, but he spurning such assistance, made a second attempt and by means of a friendly push from some of the bystanders got firmly established . . . it was a queer affair altogether but we went on very well with the help of our landlord who trotted by our side, buying now and then a halfpenny worth of cord to mend the crupper, the traces etc. *(13th July 1824)*

As the party on their 'merry and a pretty ride' travel towards Carmarthen, Margaret comments, as did Millicent Bant, on what she regards as the 'odd' way the Welsh have of whitewashing everything so that 'their cottages, roofs and all look as if covered with fresh snow, nay even the trunks of some of the trees were whitewashed'. In Carmarthen she is taken into 'a neat little farmhouse where the mistress took us into her clean dairy and gave us some excellent milk'; she sees 'cockles ready boiled and shelled selling in enormous quantities', as well as her first coracles. She certainly:

Coracles

> . . . feels no inclination to trust myself to such frail vehicles as they appear to be. They bring them down to the river on their shoulders, each man with one. They throw them very dexterously into the water and then getting in themselves, paddle away with one oar which is generally used in front of the boat and serves to steer by also. These coracles always go in pairs one on each side of the river and a net from one to the other so that the poor sewin [large salmon-like fish found in Welsh rivers] have no chance of escape. *(14th July 1824)*

Tenby, where she stays for three nights, is Margaret's next stop. She finds it 'beautifully situated', although it is a 'narrow queer place . . . having the sea almost on every side' but where 'bad, close, hot smells prevail'. Margaret clearly has as much, if not more, of a love for the sea than for mountains, for next day she has a:

> . . . delightful day in prowling about and doing nothing; charming sands for low water, capital rocks for watching the waves. We sat this evening for hours moving from rock to rock as the water displaced us. I never anywhere saw the sea rise as suddenly as it does here. One is standing in quiet possession of a vast sheet of sand one moment and then a wave comes rolling on, hardly allowing one time to look for a safe haven. There are such innumerable bays that one must be careful not to be penned in. *(15th July 1824)*

She enjoys her beach day so much that the next day, 'a glorious one', she is again tempted 'onto the rocks before breakfast . . . the drains are a terrible nuisance and the children the dirtiest and vulgarest I almost ever saw, yet one cannot help admiring their pretty faces and curling hair'. Later in the day she goes for a sail in the bay, and again waxes enthusiastic about the rocks, for they are 'quite what they ought to be, bold and rugged, covered with shells, with innumerable chasms to explore. Watched the waves all the evening, and began to think the town did not smell so close'. From the delights of the seaside, she travels inland to Llandeilo, a town she finds dirty with 'our Inn particularly close, with polished oak floors, a sight I always dislike seeing at an inn'.

Margaret is now back to daily travelling for, after this overnight stop in Llandeilo, she journeys to Brecon and the 'delightful Castle Inn' for one night and then travels southwards down the vale of Neath. The day was intensely hot and 'Sarah's accident had so damped our waterfall ardour that we left them all . . . except one about three miles from Neath [Aberdulais] that was very near the road. The body of water is very trifling, but the rocks fine and a mill adjoining is extremely picturesque'. At Neath comes:

> . . . the end of the beauties. A thick smoke closed the scene and we drew in copper at every breath. It is almost sacrilege to profane such a vale with their black roads and iron railways, but they always seem to

choose the richest spots for their infernal deed . . . [once] a sweet spot, now black roads with blacker people, tall chimneys instead of trees, brown smoke, a barren hill with the white cottages looking like so much linen hung out to dry scattered over it, form the landscape and a contrast indeed it is to the sweet vale and bold hills that are at intervals seen thro' the dense brown clouds. *(19th July 1824)*

Swansea is little better, for when she arrives it is 'all smoke . . . I can hardly fancy that the smoke covered space before one is what I have heard compared with the Bay of Dublin'. Even the Mackworth Arms where she stays is full of 'fumes of brandy and water, doors blowing and coaches setting off, but clean'. Margaret happily takes a dip in the sea before breakfast, though gives no details of whether she was in a mixed sex group of the kind that had so shocked Sarah Wilmot in 1795.

Margaret now follows the well-travelled route eastwards stopping at all the usual tourist spots. At Margam, she comments rather dryly that the owner 'the late Mr Talbot built the orangery and church and preserved the ruins from further decay and then found that he had come to the end of his purse and soon after his life'. After the weeks of rain in north Wales there has been a real change in the weather and at the **Pyle Inn** Margaret writes that it is 'very hot, no rain for more than a week . . . enjoyed a quiet stroll after breakfast across the fields. Sat upon a gate and drank in the sea breezes for the last time'. She is disappointed in the Vale of Glamorgan, having perhaps had her head turned with too much wild scenery, for she finds that although it is 'fine and rich with pretty villages and distant views of the sea . . . it is not be compared with the rich vales that we have seen'. Cardiff also disappoints, for having walked down to a lock on the canal in order to see a fine view she finds that, 'after boiling for more than a mile through all the dirt and smoke of a seaport we found, such a mist had come over the sea as to render our further walk useless'. There is more smoke at Merthyr Tydfil where the iron works are 'all smoke and coals. These are the most extensive iron works in the kingdom and there is here an overshot wheel of a most prodigious size'. From industrial Merthyr Tydfil, Margaret leaves the smoke behind her and travels to Brecon where she meets 'Mr Clarkson . . . still engaged in his laborious exertions for the poor Africans'. This would have been Thomas Clarkson who was an active abolitionist, travelling the country for over two years, gathering evidence of the trade and support for his campaign. Margaret's next stop is Crickhowell which she thinks:

> . . . the most desirable place for a residence of any that I have seen in Wales. Such high bold hills, such noble woods, such rich luxuriant corn fields & pastures, such a beautiful little river, and moreover such pretty looking gentlemen's houses dotted over the sides of the valley form altogether a more attractive spot than any we have met with in the whole course of our journey through these sweet vales. *(23rd July 1824)*

Abergavenny and the Skirrid (Sarah Wilmot, 1802)

Margaret does not stop there for long, but rides on to Abergavenny, where there is a glimpse of one of the practicalities of travelling, for she is 'detained till one o'clock by a breach of promise in our washerwoman. We set off at last with some things ironed, some things not'. She continues to enjoy the landscape all the way from Abergavenny to Monmouth, finding Raglan Castle 'the most picturesque' she has ever seen, and enjoying the views of the hills, which were 'glowing in the golden mist of a setting sun and never appeared more beautiful'.

Margaret ends her extensive visit to Wales with the ever popular Wye tour. Looking down at the Wye from the Kymin she thinks it 'hardly appeared beautiful enough for the two days we mean to devote to it, but of course my tone will change when I am actually upon it and it is only from that height that I look down with contempt on all beneath me'. She is right, for she has 'a sweet row down to Monmouth' and at lunchtime, when the oarsmen stop rowing, they spread out their provisions and float 'quietly down with the current . . . enjoyed our dinner doubly, from the novelty and the sweet stillness of the scene'. Margaret gives some interesting details about the boat itself. She travels in the Prince of Denmark, one of the regular pleasure boats provided for tourists 'with two men to row and one to steer . . . £1.2s.0d. is the price of a boat from Ross to Monmouth . . . they expected two to three shillings amongst them'. She also finds that the steersman's son was:

> . . . an artist. He showed us some of his drawings and was anxious for us to purchase one. He draws so well that I should think he must be a teacher of drawing. It seemed odd to hear our boatmen recommending me to attempt something more than pencil and to see him standing over me when I was sketching and telling me that I was beginning it

too large. He was a very intelligent young man. His father was a careful and civil man. (*27th July 1824*)

The tide allows little time for Margaret to savour Tintern, but she enjoys more time at Piercefield, forgetting 'all fatigues in the magnificence of the view. It is I think the most extensive I ever saw and at the same time rich, wild and even grand . . . we came down the cliff by a mossy staircase'. Their tour ends happily in Chepstow and on the next day Margaret leaves for England, arriving home a week later, where she ends her diary with the same sort of happy, optimistic comment that characterises it throughout, for:

> . . . it is a pleasant thing to look back upon a journey and be convinced as we are now that we have left nothing unseen. No one I am sure ever took a journey into Wales who saw more or had fewer or slighter drawbacks to their perfect enjoyment than we have had, and the remembrance of our enjoyment will always remain. (*28th July 1824*)

In summing up her visit, the rain and wet walks, the accident at the waterfall, the unpleasant smells at Swansea, the industrial pollution and other discomforts are all forgotten. Like so many travellers before and after her Margaret Martineau remembers a land in which the people are civil and courteous and the landscape is rich beyond belief, so that she too must have felt that she had spent a good part of her month in her own piece of paradise.

Tintern village (Sarah Wilmot, 1802)

Chapter 6

The Honeymoon Diarist:
Elizabeth Bower's eight-week honeymoon tour around England, Wales and Ireland (1837)

The moon shone most beautifully, & shed such a mild silvery light on the surrounding scenery . . . at half past twelve we arrived at Brecon, but everyone in the town was gone to bed, & it was not without infinite pains & a noise that seemed to me sufficient to wake the dead, that we succeeded in arousing a surly chambermaid, & persuading her to prepare a room for us, & get us some hot water. These knotty points once accomplished we were not long in resigning ourselves to Morpheus & soon forgot all our fatigues.   14th July 1837

* * *

Travellers today can arrive at our smarter hotels at any time of day or night and expect to find someone on duty. The early travellers to Wales would usually be so exhausted after several hours travel in a jolting carriage that they would be ready to stop, together with their tired horses, at an inn early in the evening and 'night' staff would not have been needed. On the rare occasions when travellers did arrive late they could well find, as did Elizabeth and Henry Bower, that they had to rouse the sleeping and disgruntled staff from their beds. Their midnight arrival at Brecon was part of a gruelling eight-week honeymoon in which they travelled nearly every day, visiting Somerset, Gloucestershire, Worcestershire, Warwickshire, north Wales, going by sea to and from Dublin, then on through south Wales before returning home to Somerset.

Elizabeth Syndercombe Fox (8 September 1807 – 25 September 1874), a vicar's daughter, married her very own vicar, the Revd Henry Tregonwell Bower, at **Symondsbury** in Dorset on the 22nd of June 1837, two days after the accession of Queen Victoria. Elizabeth was thirty years of age, slightly older than her husband, and in comfortable financial circumstances when she married. An indenture made at the time shows that she had about £300 a year income from annuities invested in her name;[1] whilst in 1866 she inherited **Fontmell Parva** in Dorset, a lovely house dating from the mid-seventeenth century. Their only child, Henry, was born two years later.

Little else is known about Elizabeth's life but, from the bequests made in her will, she would seem to have been a caring employer. She is at pains, having ensured that her immediate family were cared for, to make bequests to those who looked after her during her final illness, as well as those staff who had served her well for many years. There is 'nineteen pounds nineteen

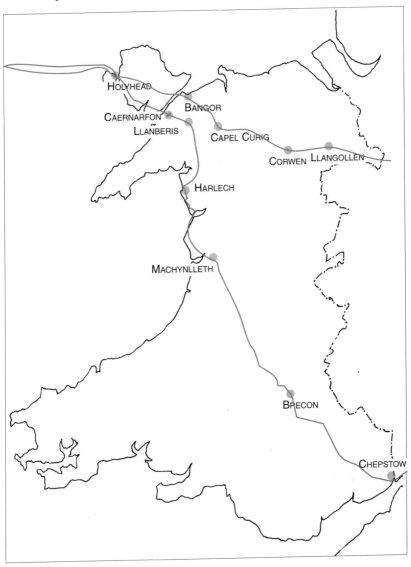

1837: A honeymoon tour through part of England, into north Wales and on to Ireland and then back to England via mid and south Wales.

shillings as an acknowledgement of his skill and attention during my illness' to her surgeon, Decimus Curne. To her coachman John Harvey she leaves £50, and to her maid Mary Jones £25. The reason for the difference in the amounts is that her coachman had given her most faithful attention for twenty-seven years, whereas Mary Jones had not served quite as well or as long. However, in a later codicil she left Mary Jones another £25 'for her attention to me during my illness'.[2] Elizabeth also left some lovely jewellery – 'a gold bracelet bought in Jerusalem, a pink topaz brooch, a twisted gold necklace, a flat ring set with emeralds and diamonds, a ring set with three pearls', and so on – giving the impression that she probably enjoyed being fashionable, as well as being a vicar's wife.

But to return to the beginning when, 'on this happy June day', Elizabeth leaves for her honeymoon after a 'parting and ceremony which were alike pleasing & wonderful to take a tour with my newly acquired husband'. Mary, no doubt a forebear of the Mary Jones of the will, also travels with them. Their first stop in Wales is at Wrexham, where they find themselves in the midst of a general election. They are staying in an inn where:

> . . . a large party of voters dining in the house rather retarded our meal but as the master of the inn had zealously exerted his influence on the Conservative side; our patriotism forbade our regretting any trifling inconvenience. The mob in the street were rather riotously disposed & Mary saw one of them deliberately open the window of a room in which a gentleman's dinner had been laid & make off with the dish of beef steak furnished for him. What he thought of its departure I never heard. (*28th June 1837*)

After dinner, Elizabeth admires some monuments in the 'handsome & neatly kept church' including one by 'Roubiliac to a Mrs Myddleton, the design of which is singular & excellent; the other to a Sir Foster Cuncliffe, remarkable for having been cut out of a block of Bath stone by a common Welsh mason'. Both these monuments, one by a famous sculptor and one by a local and probably rather rustic stonemason, commemorated well-known local people. Mrs Myddleton had lived at nearby Chirk Castle; whilst Sir Foster had been the third baronet of **Acton Park** where he had created new parkland and where, other than being an enthusiastic archer and a founder member of the Royal Society of British Bowmen, he had lived a tranquil life in this quiet part of north Wales.

On this first day of their honeymoon, Elizabeth and Henry travel in the dark to Llangollen with 'a pair of rather fanciful horses' and Elizabeth is well able to see 'the fires from the coal mines to much greater advantage than we could have done by day. The effect is very striking of a number of fires blazing in all directions & illuminating the parts immediately around them'.

When they arrive they find that:

> . . . [the inn] proved to contain every comfort we could wish to say

nothing of two very pretty girls . . . one of them, in escorting Henry about, fell over our imperial [a trunk that fitted on the roof of a carriage] & put out her elbow & I fear the poor thing suffered much during the night, but was doing well when we came away . . . one of my earliest childhood wishes was gratified, in hearing a Welsh harper . . . I then felt myself in Wales! *(28th June 1837)*

Time does not allow them to visit both Dinas Brân and Valle Crucis and a gentle visit to Valle Crucis, rather than scrambling over Dinas Brân, wins the day. Elizabeth is pleased with her choice for it is:

> . . . so perfectly shut out from the world . . . & besides which we were shown there by a perfect model of what an old woman should be, enthusiastic in her admiration of every part of the ruin & anxious to make visitors equally pleased with it. But above all expressing feelings of contentment, quite delightful to hear & affording a useful lesson to many who are surrounded by every comfort & luxury. *(29th June 1837)*

From here Elizabeth travels along the Vale of Llangollen, where 'the beauty of the scenery far surpasses my humble powers of description . . . it appeared even more beautiful than I could have imagined'. The inn at Cernioge also pleases for Elizabeth and Henry have 'a very nicely dressed dinner . . . & did not enjoy it the less for having our ears regaled during the repast by another old Welsh harper'. From Cernioge they travel on to be confronted with 'sublime & lofty' mountains, as well as waterfalls, stopping to see one 'where water appeared to gush literally from the rock'; another which 'tossed and foamed most beautifully' and a third which 'is a sheet of water forcing its way over large rocks & dashing its spray to some height . . . the crowning feature to all the other grand & picturesque points . . . [it] almost made one exclaim aloud with pleasure "These are thy glorious works of good, parent Almighty"'. Elizabeth also experiences the Welsh rain, for she is 'treated with many showers of rain & before we arrived at Capel Curig it had set in steadily'. It is perhaps not surprising that at the inn 'the people looked all as dismal as need be'. She only stops there briefly, presumably to change horses, and travels on seeing 'only barrenness' and hearing 'nothing but wind & rain . . . a tremendous night . . . [we] were thankful to reach Bangor safely & to get a comfortable reception at the Penrhyn Arms'. Here she finds, as did earlier travellers, that at the inn 'the servants speak very good English to us but chatter in Welsh to each other & I can scarcely fancy that I am still in the British Isles when I hear such an unintelligible jargon all around me'.

She is in Bangor on a Sunday so goes to church, arriving a little after the service begins so that she is nearly locked out but, 'thanks to the civility of a man who unlocked it for us, got into a nice pew just behind the Bishop . . . an interesting & benignant looking person who read the communion service & pronounced the blessing in a fine clear voice'. She goes again in the evening to the Welsh service and finds that, by using the English hymn book, she is able to 'follow the prayers, psalms & responses perfectly, but for the singing & the sermon [we] were completely at a loss. It must be a very difficult language to pronounce & the reading & preaching of it appeared a great exertion to the clergyman', no doubt a reference to the prevalence at that time of English clergy who could not speak Welsh. Another aspect of Welshness that intrigues her is the dress of the women, and she finds it diverting to her English eyes to see women 'in men's hats, many of them with long, dark cloth cloaks even in the summer season . . . all the women's hats look as if just out of the shop, it would be worth while to learn their receipt for keeping them so new'.

By the time Elizabeth arrives in Bangor the Menai Bridge had been open for twelve years and, when she visits it, she finds it precisely matched the view she had formed of it from prints and drawings, 'except in being higher from the water than I expected. High as it appears in the distance, you are astonished on discovering on a nearer view how strong it really is . . . more so . . . than is necessary in order to provide against the casualties of violent storms'.

Not all visitors begin and end their journeys to Wales on dry land. There is the Wye to row down, the Severn to cross by ferry and, for the visitor bound for Ireland, the Irish Sea to contend with. Although entry into Wales down the Wye was generally affected by nothing worse than bad weather, the same cannot be said for the other watery journeys, and Elizabeth has trying experiences of both. From Bangor she crosses the Menai Strait to Anglesey and then rides to Holyhead in order to go by sea to Ireland. On her return, a week later, she is at first lulled into a false sense of security by a calm sea and a delightfully shining sun, so begins:

> . . . [my] aquatic career in style, first taking two slight sketches of the rapidly receding shore & then standing with Henry at the bow of the vessel & watching the magnificent waves breaking beneath us till two wettings cooled my ardour & sent me astern. But all this enjoyment was not destined to be of very long duration for . . . I was taken suddenly worse & was obliged to take myself with all speed to the sofa in the cabin . . . the sea became very rough & for some time I dare not raise my head from my pillow but after a while recovered enough to laugh at my many companions in misfortune, especially at the appearance of Mary at the bottom of the stairs attended by the steward who was holding a basin under her nose with as much composure as if it had been a plate of bread & butter! *(8th July 1837)*

The relief of being back on dry land in Holyhead must have been enormous, but Elizabeth continues to feel 'the rocking and rolling of the steam packet' for quite some time. She is, however, fully recovered by the time she reaches Caernarfon where the **New Bridge Arms** 'afforded us a magnificent sitting room & every comfort' including 'a delicately roasted chicken & its appurtenances'. It is interesting that Elizabeth finds the Welsh inns far superior to the Irish ones, for 'here everything is as clean & neat as heart can desire, whereas even at our small hotel in Dublin, it was not advisable to inspect too narrowly the quantity of dust etc. etc. collected in all corners of the rooms'. It is clear that by this period most inns are much improved and it is only the occasional bad inn that comes in for criticism, such as a later one at Harlech which is a 'miserable affair compared with others we have lately inhabited, but it is right that we should not always live in luxury, lest our ideas become more high & mighty than is wise or right'.

At Caernarfon Castle she wonders how 'Kings & Queens ever managed to inhabit it without dying of the dismals', as the rooms are all so small with windows that admit very little light and 'I am one,' she says, who 'does not hold with shutting out more of the glorious sunshine than necessary for the complexion of curtains, carpets & such like'. The following day Elizabeth sets out to Llanberis in order to fulfil 'her dearest wish' of climbing Snowdon. Like Mary Anne Hibbert before her, her account is interesting enough to make it worth quoting almost in its entirety. Having fortified themselves with the 'important affair' of lunch on arrival at Llanberis, she and Henry set off:

> . . . dear Henry on a farmer's strong animal, & I on a little bay pony called Polly, as gentle as a lamb & sure-footed as a goat. The ascent . . . proved far better than we expected. Henry rode to the point within a quarter of a mile of the summit where the horses are always left, but as I felt rather giddy I was obliged to dismount & climb the steepest part on my own feet. Our guide William Williams was a very interesting character, exhibiting great intelligence & extreme good nature & attention with perfect simplicity. He beguiled the length of time devoted to the ascent by explaining the meaning of many of the Welsh names & by pointing out the peculiarities of the mountain & amused us a little with his minute account of the manner in which different kinds of food affected him.
>
> From the moment we left our ponies till we attained the very summit of the mountain we had little to do but climb crags like staircases & when we first reached the top all below was obscured in mist but gradually it cleared away on each side & gave us a more favourable view than most travellers obtain . . . magnificent indeed it was, far surpassing all description but a scene that will long dwell in the storehouse of memory. The majestic height of our position towering ever over other lofty mountains . . . was peculiarly calculated to strike any beholder with awe & bring forcibly to the mind the omnipotence of the deity. I contented myself by sitting down on a heap of stones on the summit & admiring the vastness of the landscape around me but Henry, more adventurous, must needs mount on a wooden pillar raised above the stones, & was insufferably conceited at having thus occupied a more elevated position than myself.

> When we talked of descending, William Williams with all the activity of
> a chamois, jumped from one crag to another & almost before we could
> watch his motions had reached the bottom of a deep perpendicular
> precipice to procure for me two different sorts of saxifrage & a plant
> called the alpine sow-wort which has only been found on Snowdon in
> the last year or two . . . we had a splendid view of the sunset behind a
> distant mountain . . . my pretty little Polly was waiting for me as we
> regained our track & when I gave her a parting pat on dismounting at
> the inn door, I much wished that I could have conjured her home with
> me for she seemed in every way qualified for the honour of belonging
> to a lady but the distance from Dorset was too great to think of
> purloining her. Right glad was I to find myself once more on a sofa for
> tho' very proud of my achievement in having been at the tip top of
> Snowdon, I think I never felt so tired in my life, & stiff as a poker too
> with riding & scrambling. We had been absent more than five hours, &
> the instant I had swallowed some dinner I repaired to rest but could get
> no sleep for visions of precipices & huge stones. (10th July 1837)

Their guide on this climb was one of the most famous of all the Snowdon
mountain guides. Nick-named 'Will Boots', he was a keen botanist, and it
was on a search for a rare plant that he fell to his death in 1861 when he was
only fifty-six years old.

Despite her exhaustion after this climb Elizabeth and Henry set off next
day to **Harlech**, but not in style, for 'the child who rode the leader could not
certainly have washed his face since Sunday and wore his ordinary dress of
trousers, shoes & socks, & only the addition of a shield to guard his leg from
the traces'. Later she meets a 'young girl who supported her mother by her
knitting', and from whom she buys some worsted stockings. After a brief
overnight stop, Elizabeth has another long day, travelling down the coast to
Barmouth then inland to Dolgellau and south to Machynlleth, where she
arrives, not surprisingly, 'tired and sleepy'. She has expected to find another
good inn, as this has generally been her experience in Wales, but she finds
herself in:

> . . . one which I should think had never before been honoured by the
> presence of a gentleman & lady. Certain it is that the waiter started as
> if he had been shot when asked for an upstairs sitting room & that
> various matters in the upper regions set me shrieking with laughter in
> the face of the attendant. However, after some contrivance & sundry
> alterations, we managed to make ourselves pretty comfortable, & I
> take some credit to myself for writing my dear uncle a very long letter
> in spite of my fatigue before we retired to bed. *(12th July 1837)*

It is astonishing how cheerful these women travellers remain in the face of
both the major and minor obstacles that beset them, and equally astonishing
how little, given the amount of travelling and sightseeing they do each day,

they complain of fatigue. Yet tiredness does beset most of them occasionally and Elizabeth is no exception for the next day, a Sunday, she finds 'the bustle of the last week obliged me to make this in every sense a day of rest, & finding the afternoon service would be in Welsh, I did not even attempt to leave the house, but read at home'. After this brief day of rest Elizabeth has her marathon day when she travels from Machynlleth to Brecon, but the following morning, 'in spite of our late travelling last night, we arose in good time feeling that many miles remained to be accomplished'. On this day she and Henry travel to Abergavenny, Usk and finally to Chepstow, from where she leaves Wales. However, her departure is the occasion of her second aquatic adventure for, 'having seized a few sandwiches & hastened to ferry at the Old Passage [one of two ferry crossings before the advent of the Severn bridges]', she and Henry find that it was:

> . . . a matter of doubt whether the tide would admit of our crossing before the expiration of an hour & half, the idea of which delay was anything but agreeable. However, after much discussion, we were told that if we went we must start at once, so with great glee we jumped on board the Duke of Beaufort steamer, which malgré her grand name, looked so crazy that I almost expected she would either blow up or fall to pieces before we could possibly land. Land indeed we did not for the height of the water at the proper pier was somehow or other not suitable to the vessel, so we were popped out, carriage & all, close under the cliffs & almost in the water. A pair of horses from the Aust ferry inn were there to meet us, & with one wheel literally covered by the sea, we were dragged to the inn, where we had a comfortable meal of tea & cold meat, & then set forth lighted by the same 'gentle moon' which had so added to our enjoyment last night. *(15th July 1837)*

Chepstow (Sarah Wilmot, 1802)

After this rather ignominious departure from Wales, Elizabeth returns to her new home with her new husband. In her travel journal, other than references to her 'dear Henry', Elizabeth says nothing about her newly married status but, as she nears the end of her honeymoon, she confides her innermost feelings to her diary. She is clearly full of apprehension about her new status fearing that she might not conduct herself as she ought towards the 'family & friends of my dear husband'. The closer she gets to her new home the more her feelings of fear grow and 'in this state of depression, it was most soothing to receive a kind welcome'. She resolves to make herself acceptable to her new in-laws '& not to give them cause to regret that their son is removed from their fireside'. Such a kind welcome seems to revive her usual optimistic mood, for her diary ends on a happy note. 'Thus', she says, 'ended a delightful tour which occupied eight weeks & two days & not only afforded us great present pleasure, but I think will be pleasing to reflect on . . . Finis'.

And so Elizabeth Bower returns to a new life and new duties. She seems, in many ways, to be very much like Sarah Wilmot: a serious woman with a social conscience but also a sense of fun, as well as the good fortune to be blessed with a comfortable income, a lovely home and what sounds as though it will be a happy marriage. Whether she ever returned to Wales is not known, but her lively accounts of aspects of her travels, in particular her ascent of Snowdon, remain another gem of early travel writing about Wales.

Chapter 7

"Our Fortnight in Wales":
Frederica Rouse Boughton (1860)

It was almost like the people in Pilgrims Progress, to get to this snug place & to be welcomed by such a dear woman as Mrs. Jones . . . she is very tall, & spare, & with a delightful quaint effect about her. Really, speaking without prejudice, she is very good looking, & such a sweet expression & kind, obliging manner. She always wore dark bright blue cotton with large, white spots, made in the most old-fashioned way, & very quaint. Notwithstanding these peculiarities she was not old by any means & most fascinating. She won upon us immediately by her ladylike manner, & her pretty Welsh accent, sounding rather foreign.   25th August 1860

* * *

Most of the early travellers to Wales, grand though some of them might have been, stayed in inns as they rattled round Wales in their carriages. Frederica is another kind of tourist, for she stays in Dolgellau in what nowadays would be regarded as bed and breakfast accommodation and makes daily excursions from there.

There is something exciting about saving the best until last. *Our Fortnight in Wales*, written as part of Frederica Rouse Boughton's diary of her daily life in 1860, is the liveliest of all the travel diaries found in the archives, a beautifully illustrated diary which recounts the holiday adventures of a party of young people. It fizzes with the fun, excitement and sheer pleasure of being alive, and although Frederica simply describes her day-to-day jaunts, in doing so she also conjures up a paradise of beautiful landscape, friendly people and fun-filled days in such a way that her diary is worth reproducing almost verbatim.

Frederica was born on the 15th of April 1838, nine months after the accession of Queen Victoria. She was the fifth daughter of Sir William Rouse Boughton of **Downton Hall**, Herefordshire, and Charlotte Knight, a daughter of Thomas Andrew Knight. Thomas Knight was a founder of the Royal Horticultural Society and his experiments had a far-reaching impact on British horticulture. His brother Richard Payne Knight, as one of the most renowned exponents of the Picturesque movement, had an effect on the aesthetic taste of the period. Thus, with a baronet for a father and renowned intellectuals on her mother's side, Frederica was born into a background of privilege and culture. Despite this her childhood was not altogether happy, as her mother died when she was four, leaving the eight children in the care of a father who was alleged to have been something of a tyrant.

In 1861, a year after her Welsh holiday, Frederica married Richard Orlebar, whom she clearly loved very deeply, for she says 'if I tried to describe my husband, or to speak of the quiet, happy life he has led me these last three years since we have been married, I would utterly fail . . . we have had some little troubles, as every human being must, just to make us sure we were not enjoying a pleasant dream but walking on solid earth!' And writing about Richard on her return from a period of convalescence she says 'I was too happy to speak when I saw my dear husband again . . . I knew I must look very undemonstrative to please him while I was in public, & I am sure we both acted our parts to perfection . . . [but] how quickly the ice melted when the spectators were gone'. After her marriage Frederica moved to her husband's home in Bedfordshire where they and their two sons enjoyed an affluent life, at least until the agricultural depression of 1873, when their comfortable existence was shattered. They were left in comparative poverty, and often had to appeal to wealthier members of the family for financial help. Frederica died in her ninetieth year on the 24th of February 1928, having outlived both her husband and all her brothers and sisters.

Our Fortnight in Wales begins when Frederica sets out for north Wales on the 24th of August 1860. She travels with her two sisters Theresa and Mary; a Mrs Russell; and her children Katy, Gertrude, Sophy and Lechmere. At the time of their adventures in Wales, Frederica is twenty-two, her sisters a few years older and Lechmere is twenty-three. What Lechmere feels about being the only male in a group consisting of his mother and six delightfully giddy-sounding young women is never revealed. Although Frederica was a seasoned traveller – she had undertaken continental trips and visited Scotland – she had not become blasé and the whole of her Welsh diary brims over with excitement. Before they set out, on the basis that Wales being so 'foreign' would lack the basic necessities, Frederica and her sisters take a 'belt and braces' approach to the trip. First there is the cooking:

> . . . oh the cakes – what an effect they produced as they came, five in number, out of the oven, & were put on a tray with all the other contents of the hamper for our inspection before packing. We had poked into the hamper every available article that we thought wd. be scarce at Dolgelly, fruit & vegetables (even pepper & salt) & as much jam & marmalade as the hamper seemed likely to take without remonstrance. (*23rd August 1860*)

Then there is the sewing, 'stitching vehemently at a store of small things which no-one else cd. help me with, such as strings on my sketching bag, fingers of gloves, & heaps of small etceteras' and the packing when 'all the roughest, most enduring sort of clothes were pulled out, & the thickest of boots, & old skirts & jackets, which had evidently seen service on many such occasions'.

They travel into Wales by steam train, arriving at Llangollen Road Junction in teeming rain. Whilst the women of the party huddle in a shed by the line, Lechmere comes into his own by looking after all thirteen pieces of luggage. They then travel on by omnibus in high spirits, chattering all the way and getting their first glimpse of the Welsh hills with their 'bare, unclothed look . . . all green & slippery looking & bare from top to bottom, only sometimes with a little topping of heather in a pretty purple sheet, contrasting with the smooth hillsides'. As it is far too late for them to go onto Dolgellau they find comfortable rooms at the **Kings Head** in Llangollen, where they hear a Welsh harper and have a wonderful tea, which of course includes many of the things they had packed:

> . . . we never laughed more than over tea that night, being a very large party and a very small room, we were always tumbling over each other whenever we moved, and besides, we were in such high spirits that it did not take much to make us laugh. It was such a wonderful tea for a hotel, including jam, marmalade, & honey, & all sorts of odds and ends . . . there was a woman outside playing the harp, Jenny Jones etc. Not knowing whether she was doing this as an amateur or professionally we were doubtful whether she wd. be offended at us offering to pay her, & so had to relieve our minds by occasionally getting up & saying something civil to her, all of which remarks she took in such a perfectly stolid business like way that we decided a shilling wd. save us all the trouble of complimenting, and we consequently finished our tea in peace. (*24th August 1860*)

The next day there is only a morning free before the next stage of the journey, but Frederica does not let a moment go by unused, so visits *both* Castell Dinas Brân and Valle Crucis. One of Frederica's charms is that she and her friends often have only the vaguest of ideas about how to get to their destination and, as a result, spend much of their time wandering about in a hopeful rather than a knowledgeable manner. Such is their trip to Valle Crucis, but when they get lost and ask local people the way, she reports that they can only say 'Dim Sasenag'. When they eventually find the ruined abbey it stands:

> . . . very well in the old valley, planted there snugly with fine old trees close to it, & hills rising all round. We all sat down on a wall outside the west end by way of taking a 'first impression' & it was certainly very pretty. The old grey stone told so well against the trees, all in patches of colour & weather stains . . . there was . . . a very modern bell which we rang & a gaunt looking woman with a red shawl & flowers in her bonnet appeared to let us in. She was a character this woman, looking so very hard & disapprovingly at us, who were laughing & talking & I suppose not looking sufficiently impressed at the first sight of the ruins. We were however very much struck, as it happened. The ruins are

beautiful, quite so beautiful as to make one forget the fact of being a tourist, & force one to stand still & take them in thoroughly . . . we wandered about to see every nook . . . the hard-featured woman . . . seemed to consider the girl part of the party as too irreverent or incorrigible to take any notice of them, & so betook herself to Lechmere, & spoke to no-one else as long as we stayed. *(25th August 1860)*

They then climb Dinas Brân, with Frederica having:

> . . . no notion until we began to climb how high the hill really was. However, we set to manfully & kept plodding on for I am afraid to say how long in this tremendous sun . . . but when we arrived at . . . the top, the view quite repaid us . . . there are only a few fragments left now of very old masonry all in detached bits. We sat down amongst the ruins, out of reach of the hot sun, & pulled out our Black's guide which told us the supposed history of the old castle . . . there is a vulgar little shop established amongst the ruins for ginger beer etc. & which of course we, on the whole, disdained, though in my secret heart, considering the heat of the day, I might have been tempted to patronise it, if the idea had not been so universally scouted . . . we (then) discovered that we had lost the guidebook & with great difficulty we made a child understand that she shd. get 6d for running up to the castle, & bringing it down to the inn before we started. This plan answered happily, & we got back the book a day or two after we had settled at Dolgelly. *(25th August 1860)*

Back in Llangollen they decide, despite their hampers of food, to lay in a good store of biscuits and buns for their forty mile journey. The journey is not a happy one for, where Millicent Bant many years before had had an inebriated coach driver, Frederica has a cruel one:

> . . . the driver was very bad, & managed to get the poor horses knocked up at the beginning of each stage, & we were doomed to hear them continually beaten, till it was too dreadful & we positively got down for one bad hill. The front traces broke into the bargain, so that one of the leaders was unable to pull, & the remaining three wretched creatures cd. hardly get on. He made up for it by galloping downhill as fast as he cd. go, & I fd. it anything but pleasant being in an outside place. It was raining hard all the last part of the way. *(25th August 1860)*

They finally arrive in Dolgellau at 9 p.m. and walk up to their lodgings at **Brynffynnon**, where they are met by their landlady, Mrs. Jones. There is also a Mr. Jones, whom they hardly ever see, two shy young daughters, an 'uninteresting' niece and the maid, Margaret, who is 'also a character & a very pretty little thing, though dreadfully slow'. They quickly establish themselves 'very snugly, & got by degrees the boxes brought up, & unpacked partially before we got food for ourselves. It was a woeful fact that part of the contents of our . . . hamper was found the worse for wear . . . & had to be thrown away'.

Frederica begins her first day in Dolgellau by going to church and then setting out on the first of her many adventures. She begins in comparatively gentle fashion by climbing the lower slopes of Cadair Idris but she quickly gets into difficulties:

> I meant to do something quite original & thought I was finding such a much superior path for myself through the bogs & stones than anyone else had discovered, but after clambering on for some time, I found myself hopelessly stuck in some bushes, & saw all the others trooping up to the rescue, shouting with amusement at my absurd dilemma . . . there are great walls built right across the tumbled country to keep the sheep in, composed of great stones, all the top ones being loose, & so high as to be generally above the level of our heads . . . these stone walls are dangerous, as one might so easily, in getting over, roll off a few loose stones, which must crush one's ankle if they happened to fall on it. *(26th August 1860)*

Over the next two days Frederica and her friends do first the **Torrent** and then the **Precipice Walk**. They go well armed with provisions taking 'amongst other things the cheese, one of the gingerbread cakes, a good lump of cold beef, and all sorts of etceteras, for we knew by experience how ravenous we all became on these occasions'. Lunch comes before the walk and the whole party is:

> . . . so very quaint and funny, all perched up inside and outside this strange affair like rooks – everyone saying something at each minute more absurd than the last – handing in & out the provisions & the wonderful cheese . . . when luncheon was over, the knives cleaned & everything perfectly tidy, we thought it was time to start for the Precipice Walk . . . taking the man with us to carry cloaks etc. It is quite a rough path though broad and with great logs of timber in the way which we amused ourselves jumping over, & soon we came to a pretty still little lake which was so picturesque . . . we went on our way & came to a high stone wall right across the path, over which a queer little ladder had been contrived . . . it is only a little path, a few feet broad, & strewn over with quantities of rubble from the rocks above . . . a turn in the hill took us off this narrow path, literally the Precipice Walk . . . all tumbled, stony & heathery, & dotted with branches of juniper. Our spirits rose, & we gave them vent by all running headlong down the other side of the hill . . . Cader was just turning a dark blue, with the evening shadows coming down, & the air gradually getting colder, but huddled up in our cloaks, we cared little for the cold. *(28th August 1860)*

For their next adventures they decide to visit three well-known waterfalls: Rhaeadr Ddu, **Rhaeadr Mawddach** and **Pistyll Cain**. As always they take provisions, although they are rather mundane compared with their usual feasts, consisting only of a 'huge lump of bread & a hard-boiled egg apiece'. When they near the falls a guide presents himself and they accept his services, thinking it would be silly to get lost having ridden all that way. They set off demurely enough but soon come to some copper workings where they have to ride through a noisy yard with machinery clanking away. At this point Frederica nearly has a neck-breaking adventure, as:

> . . . the pony refused & kept backing. Now the path being narrow & a straight descent to the river on the right, the horrible idea seized me that we shd. both go backing over the precipice . . . I roared with all my strength bringing up Gertrude & Mary full tilt to my assistance . . . by that time the pony had come to the wise conclusion that it was better to have the machinery roaring in front than me roaring on his back & he quickly proceeded, passing the wheels quietly. *(29th August 1860)*

Eventually they tie the ponies to a tree, and follow a path which brings them out by Pistyll Cain, but 'on the way down to the fall, Mary & I were jumping over a stream together & the jolt shook her egg, which she was just preparing to devour out of her pocket. It went away, straight into the stream'. However, when they were packing their picnics, Frederica with 'becoming forethought [had] tucked in an egg extra to the others, & as it turned out, it was a very useful precaution' for Mary is now able to have her lunch after all. Having admired this very fine fall with 'a good deal of larch or fir which always makes a pretty feathery effect over water' they go scrambling through some brushwood to Pistyll Mawddach:

> . . . on emerging from which the fall burst suddenly upon us & it was beautiful . . . the water runs through quantities of small rocks with shingly sorts of shores. It comes dashing gloriously down from the heights all in foam, looking so clear & bright & in the shadows just varying in tints according to the colour of the rocks it flows over . . . as I was packing up my sketching things, I heard a shout of "Oh such a pretty little cave" & there it was, not far from where we had been sitting, the entrance to a little cave in the side of the hill, almost buried in the luxuriant fern & heather that grew round the entrance. Right before the mouth the water dripped constantly like a sparkling veil, so plentifully that we could only just see inside. We all looked in but cd. see nothing. . . . on reaching the road, we got rid of the man, as we considered we cd. quite find our way to the third fall Rhayader Ddu, without him . . . we must have looked so very picturesque winding up the steep path to the third fall, a tribe of ponies make such a good foreground, we mostly walking as the ascent was very steep & pulling them up after us. They were all varieties of colour & one had a peculiar

coloured mane that shone bright amber in the sun & made the funniest effect on its dark coat. They were such a rough, untidy, picturesque lot; some of them boasting bright bunches of mountain ash in their bridles, with the glorious scarlet berries making a lovely headdress!

The path was so lovely all in odd shaped slabs of stone & loose ground enclosed between an old wall on one side & a high rock on the other, the wall being of that thoroughly tumble to bits description that seems only put there as an excuse for ferns & mosses to sprout in, the ferns turning gold colour in the autumn & making such a lovely contrast with the dark rich green of the mosses & the tufts of purple heather. It was quite perfectly beautiful & the rock on the right not less so, a nice cracked eccentric rock with independent looking broom & heather bursting out in every crevice & then the mountain ash with the red berries & the waving fern! Oh how they must enjoy life up at that height, up in the fresh air, with something always changing, & beautiful to look at & the sound of the water torrenting down the rocks in the distance. Everything looks so alive, one can hardly fancy they have not eyes & ears to enjoy it all. As for ourselves, we never used our eyes & ears to better purpose & shouts of "Oh how very lovely" in all varieties of tones seemed to be the only relief we cd. find till we reached the top . . . we soon found the fall & were properly struck. It is a good big fall broad & white & the river runs through a fine ravine well wooded & perfectly untamed even by tourists & guidebooks best efforts. There must have been a path somewhere through the wood but as we did not light upon it, we pushed our way back as we had come. *(29th August 1860)*

After all this walking and exploring, the next day is quieter, although not entirely uneventful, for Frederica and her friends try to track down the letters that had been sent to them *Poste Restante*. This was however easier said than done, for although:

Kathy & Mary generally undertook to rescue our letters from the Post office; generally this was no easy matter. If we asked for them at the Post Office they told us "Mrs Jones little girl had just taken them". If we asked Mrs Jones we heard her little girl had called & some ladies had just taken them away. If we all separated & foraged about the town two & two after the letters, we always heard at the Post Office or in some direction that some two other members of our party had got them, & when at last the different scouts all met in the market place, & attacked each other in an aggrieved undertone "Why didn't you let us know you'd got them?" the answer invariably was "We got them? We've never seen anything of them. We were expecting you to bring them" "Us? Oh dear no, we've never seen them!". So it went on, day after day, till we were quite tired of letter hunting, & let them take their chance. *(30th August 1860)*

On this occasion they do manage to get their letters, spend the morning replying to them, and then take what must have seemed a rather genteel ride (in comparison with their cantering and running down hills activities) in a donkey cart. On their return to Dolgellau they have:

> . . . an amusing encounter with a troop of small boys in all varieties of costumes & patches. They were all more or less ragged, but with such happy, mischievous faces & looking so roguish as they all pressed round us, teasing & bothering for half pennies, that they were quite irresistible & we held up a penny before them all . . . [and] tossed it in amongst the group & let them scramble for it. It was such an amusing sight that we went on throwing pennies until all our store was exhausted & throwing silver was too expensive as a form of amusement. *(30th August 1860)*

Their next big adventure is their sudden decision, when out on another donkey cart ride, to make a dash for Cadair Idris as it was looking:

> . . . much less formidable than everyone had made it out & as several of us felt very lively and up to a good deal more walking, we suddenly resolved to make a dash at it & find our way to the little dark lake . . . before we turned homeward. We thought it wd. be such fine fun to start on our own devices up Cader Idris, though of course we knew we cd. nothing like reach the top that night . . . [we] struck right across some fields, over a footbridge, across a stream, through a wood & on again. We presently came to another winding of the same stream & here we searched in vain for a bridge, but not finding one, we determined to walk through, as the stream was not much above our boots. We spent some time dancing backwards & forwards up & down the bank, in search of a convenient ford, & at last Gertrude & I discovered what we considered a properly shallow one, & went bravely across, while Lechmere & Kathy crossed somewhere out of our sight by some stepping stones. Our primitive fashion of crossing was the quickest, & I considered the safest, since I never yet trusted to stepping stones without getting a slip & ending up being much wetter than I cd. have been by simply walking through. It is also a great delusion taking off ones' shoes & stockings on these occasions as one's feet only get horribly bruised & hurt, & one stands howling half-way through the water, a miserable spectacle & a great source of amusement to everyone but oneself.

> Having all got prosperously through our difficulties, we pushed on up the hill & what a push it was! Really in places it was more like a ladder than a hill – almost straight. The ground was all broken & stony so that there was no fear of slipping but we were obliged to get a little rest occasionally on the tempting tufts of heather on our path, where we

looked back & spent some minutes 'admiring the view'!! The view was quite worth admiring . . . on the right stretched away all the Bala lake country; straight in front rose the Nannau hill & on the left we saw the sea, & a faint idea of Barmouth. It was well worth the climb, but still it must be said that the climb was extremely difficult.

We had been threatened with a great mad bull which was said to haunt the base of the mountain, & people seemed to think we shd. have done better to have taken a guide under the circumstances. The idea of taking Lewis Pugh for our champion, & making him fight the bull single handed, while we all took the opportunity of running away! What a glorious sight it cd. have been, 3 ladies & a gentleman tearing down full speed upon Dolgelly with a mad bull behind them. Happily we saw nothing of the bull, though as Gertrude & I sank down occasionally on the heather to rest, we decided it wd. be quite impossible to move past a foot's pace if we heard the bull roaring at that moment. Luckily for us the picture was only in our imagination & after a dreadfully steep two miles of climbing, & surmounting endless rises of ground, every one of which we attacked under the idea that this must be the last, & the one that concealed the lake from view, we reached the true border, & to our great satisfaction saw the lake lying deep, dark, blue & mysteriously silent in the shingly basin at our feet.

We stood on the rim of this basin watching it for some time when we discovered that Lechmere & Kathy were missing & we both shouted at once, knowing they could not be far off. Echo after echo followed amongst the rocks round the lake, & they took up our shouts so long after we had uttered them that we cd. not believe it was not strange voices answering. There is something so mocking in an echo, & so like the human voice that one hardly knows whether to be provoked, or amused, or frightened. Just at this moment I was feeling so much like the Babes in the Wood, as Gertrude & I stood sketching the dark lake & hearing those mysterious sounds all alone up there & without a human being within sight that the echo made me feel rather frightened than otherwise. Then there followed a sort of sighing round the lake for no apparent cause. I suppose it was the wind, but it sounded very strange & ghostly, coming & dying away, & altogether it had a sort of unearthly effect that was not quite pleasant. The lake is quite small but very deep & very clear, a tempting place to throw stones into as one wd. into a well . . . the water is beautifully cold & clear up at this height as we soon discovered, & it was most refreshing to find anything so good after our long, hard pull up the hill. They say it is a good 2½ miles from the road, consequently it must be fully 5½ miles from Dolgelly & these last miles on the rough ground were like double many ordinary ones. Gertrude & I, still seeing no-one, now began to shout again, & again the echoes shouted with all their might an answer. At length we were gladdened by a more human sounding shout, & at the same time Lechmere & Kathy appeared. Of course we all began at once making tourist like remarks on the lake, & both detachments of two exclaiming at once "How very stupid of you to miss us" to the other party.

We all set off as hard as we cd. go down the hill, knowing we were not yet out of reach of the great bugbear, the wild bull . . . we tore downhill at a great pace & seemed to arrive in no time at the great sheep wall that had been so hard to climb on our way up. This time we followed the one side right down into the valley, & crossed at a much easier place very near where we had forded the stream. We lighted immediately on a footbridge which it seems wonderful all our hunting had not brought to light the first time, & so we sped along at a good pace by the same path, across the 2nd winding of the stream, & then one or two fields & we were again on the road. I did not feel much tired with the hill work; it was the awful pace at which we went home that did for me. I think it must have been at more than 4 miles an hour, for I remember feeling more like a London cab horse on a wet Sunday than I had ever done before. However by hook or by crook I managed to get home but may I never have to stump along the hard road at that pace again! *(31st August 1860)*

Despite her exhaustion after this skirmish with Cadair Idris, Frederica is 'up with the lark' next day and making preparations for a day on the beach at Barmouth. Getting ready for such a trip means eating a large breakfast, collecting an 'immense amount of provisions', and taking their 'bathing apparatus'. They get to Barmouth about noon, where they settle themselves:

. . . on a sandbank in the warm sun, having all our baskets with us & resolved to stay there to eat our luncheon. We thought it wd. be well before luncheon to get our bathing over, & acting on this idea, Mary, Gertrude & I started with our bathing things under our arms & with Kathy, Theresa & Sophy to act as maids, & to warn if any human being appeared in sight on the horizon. We wandered far up the shore, & having found a nice quiet place possessed ourselves of it & were in about two minutes ready to jump in the water. It was such immense fun . . . we splashed away for about 20 minutes in the water, made vague & unsuccessful efforts to swim which came to less than nothing. Floating was almost worse, for it was impossible to lie quietly on the water without a ducking from some dashing little wave that came rushing to shore with its pretty white sparkling crest. We made the most of our time notwithstanding these drawbacks & at all events succeeded in making our three maids regret that they had not come prepared for a like amusement. The water was very pleasant, though rather rough & though we all knew it to be intensely silly staying in so long, we still pleaded to our consciences "Oh, one dip more!" & with one accord fell backwards on the water as we said so. 20 minutes was a charitable computation of time & we did feel rather cold when we came out, but we managed to dress in about 5 minutes, & walked briskly about to get warm again.

We began to feel the ends of our fingers comfortably by the time we reached the original sandbank on which we found Mrs Russell & Lechmere still seated in charge of the provision baskets. We were of course congratulated on our happy escape from drowning as Lechmere had warned us the tide was going out, & wd. most likely carry us with it, like the young ladies in the song "One wave & they were out at sea, a world of water round, poor damsels how they longed to be, once more on English ground!". The provision baskets had been well packed & though we did ample justice to their contents we had still a good deal to spare so we stacked up the remaining bread, salt etc. in a heap, & put a leg of chicken as a sort of cairn on the top, in such a conspicuous position that someone must have seen it after we left, & probably benefited by the discovery.

After luncheon we all wandered off in different directions, sketching & exploring in a very meek way the little shops in Barmouth. There was one gingerbread shop which we patronised largely, laying in a store of biscuits & cracknels to amuse us on the way home . . . we had got it into our heads that it wd. be most delightful to bathe again before we left . . . we all did come to the unanimous conclusion that we were going to do something very silly, but the idea of bathing twice in the day in this sort of excursion, was so perfectly novel that we cd. not give it up, & accompanied by our three maids & our half wet bathing things we posted off to the same place, had our dip & enjoyed it most thoroughly. After this, as it was getting late, we thought there was no time to lose . . . it was getting very cold, & we had to put on all our wraps, waterproofs & everything coming in to requisition, for before we had gone far, the rain came down heavily & it blew tremendously. However it was much the same to us, we were packed up in waterproofs with the hood up, much in the style of Macbeth's witches, & we cared very little for wet or fine. *(1st September 1860)*

Two days later, Frederica and friends set off on a pony expedition each with 'a tremendous lump of cake in our habit pockets'. They set out along the **Tywyn** road:

. . . with a sort of vague idea that we shd. make out some path which would take us over the hills to **Tallyllyn**. We had not an idea of the country, beyond a little smattering gathered from the maps, & there was something so very independent in starting thus in search of adventures that we shd. have been quite sorry for anyone to have officiously let us know where our present road wd. lead & what wd. be the shortest & most findable track to Tallyllyn . . . we looked such a picturesque cavalcade . . . the ponies all different colours & as shaggy & uncivilised a lot as cd. well be met with . . . as we turned a sharp bend in the hill a most lovely view burst upon us . . . the town of Barmouth lay in the most beautiful hazy colouring close down on the beach looking as though an unusually high tide wd. almost swallow it up – but so lovely! The opposite bank of the river is gloriously wooded, & made a good background to the sunny little town, & the sea stretched away in a delicate blue beyond it, glittering in the sun, & with hardly a wave visible.

We shouted with delight, and cd. have stayed any given time looking at this wonderful amount of beauty, but there was no time to be lost . . . we were getting very hungry, & . . . some sort of resting place was indispensable in our starving condition . . . when in addition to all this, the sun suddenly went in, the bright sky clouded over, the wind got up, & the rain began to fall rather fast, the hitherto jovial little "band of moss troopers" . . . began to lose heart, & to howl & growl with great vehemence . . . a succession of rickety gates at long intervals rather kept up our courage, as they looked more likely to exist in the vicinity of some town than in the perfectly desolate wilds where we might otherwise have supposed ourselves to be. After several gates had been passed, we suddenly came upon a group of little girls, tumbled down in picturesque attitudes in a huge bundle of dried fern, which they use all about these parts as litter for cattle. We enquired the way but of course to no effect 'Dim Sasenag' was all they cd. say, but the very sight of human beings made us feel considerably happier, & after a few minutes the sight of a white house & a garden railing set us all right again. A gate of the most unsafe description took us into a broad lane with high tangled hedges . . . we trotted on merrily through the gate at the end of the lane, & by a sharp turn, soon found ourselves in the broad high road.

By dint of a good deal of gibberish, we enquired the name of the place, & found it to be **Llanegryn** . . . on enquiring about how far we were from home, they coolly told us about 16 miles, we having already come quite that distance. The ponies seemed flagging & we began making enquiries from every creature we met as to where we cd. get corn for them & possibly food for ourselves. All their answers tended the same way. There was no sort of inn till about two miles farther on, at a little place called, as nearly as we cd. understand Llangwrool, spelt I think Llangwrl [**Llwyngwril**]. Towards this promised land we set our faces, really beginning to feel rather anxious about the distance when measured with the ponies remaining capacities & trying to calculate what sort of time we were likely to reach home. In time we reached the village . . . & by such a road. I think I never saw anything more perfectly lovely . . . the road overhangs the sea just enough to hide any bit of beach that may exist between the base of the rocks & the water, so that you look over the wall right into the blue water, looking so clear & deep, & stretching away into the horizon, with a beautiful broad track of sunlight right across it . . . & Barmouth nestled down on the shore, looking so bright & sunny in a rich, beautiful blue, much like the view we had seen in the morning, only richer & deeper in colouring. It was more like an oil painting & cd. hardly be represented with sufficient intensity in water colours. The sky, land & sea seemed all of a piece, different in actual tint, but united by a faint haze . . . by dint of a good deal of shouting in the horses ears, we reached . . . the little inn, giving up the ponies to be fed . . . some of the others showed their senses by going to little shop in the village, with uninviting buns displayed for sale, & buying a quantity of rather second-rate cracknels, clean but flabby. They were devoured eagerly & we felt all the better for them after our long ride. The ponies were now supposed to be sufficiently fed & rested for us to start again, and a very few minutes saw us mounted, & once more on our way. *(3rd September 1860)*

Despite the traumas of this ride Frederica is back on a pony again next day and, as with so many of the earlier diarists, her description of the landscape has the feel of paradise about it. There is:

. . . [a] pretty stony sort of lane, overgrown with briary hedges of luxuriant growth which looked as though they had never been tight & compact in their lives . . . having posted up at a tremendous pace, we sat down on a gate at the top for a few minutes rest, & really to enjoy the scenery & our own conversation. I certainly admit that the others had not raved a bit too much about the view. It was lovely, such ranges of distant blue hills on all sides; the ground sloped away in every direction from the hill on which we were standing, forming beautiful snug green valleys with small cottages from which rose the clear, faint blue smoke that seemed only intended to be picturesque, & not looking as if it cd. belong to a matter of fact useful fire inside. Here & there an old woman in the short bright petticoats of the country appeared at the doors. *(4th September 1860)*

On one of their trips, Sophy had struck up an acquaintance with one of the inhabitants of these small cottages and they all decide to go and see the farmhouse in which she lived:

. . . a rather a gloomy looking place . . . we crossed a little garden, of which the less said the better, & in the garden was a little bridge over a stream. The bridge was of rather a curious construction being made to flap back directly you took your foot off it, so as to look like no bridge at all, the pressure of the foot alone keeping it in its place. It was so constructed to prevent the sheep and the cattle getting over. We all went on into the old house, and the quaint aspect of the low kitchen, with its great chimney place and simmering cauldron, and the delightful old woman standing over the boiling pot struck us all with such a pleasant surprise, that Sophy, interpreting the feelings of our party, rushed forward, & clapping her hands with delight, sank down on one of the low seats in the chimney corner, shouting "Oh, what a delightful place!".

The old woman's face showed that she appreciated this unsophisticated introduction, for she made us all sit down & hurried off in search of all sorts of good things to tempt us with – oatmeal cakes, milk & buttermilk, pressing us to eat with a good deal of unintelligible Welsh, & the most unmistakeable signs & gestures. We thought it only polite that she had not been gesticulating in vain, so we nodded most graciously, & set to, she watching us with the greatest pleasure, & all on the qui vive to fetch us more supplies if we cd. have exhausted the original stock. I sketched the scene. I have put in Gertrude making an effort to resist another bowl of buttermilk which the old woman pressed upon us towards the last. The good old soul shook hands with us all round, & made more signs & more gibberish, all which we cd. only interpret as expressing the pleasure our visit had given her. The feeling was quite mutual. *(4th September 1860)*

Finally, as the culmination of her adventures, Frederica does climb Cadair Idris. The day is perfectly clear to start with but, of course, it does not last, and they soon find they are:

. . . walking straight up into a cloud . . . the fog was ever so thick, that at a very little distance, we lost sight of each other, & cd. hear the voices long before we saw who was speaking. It was a curious effect, the voice coming out of the fog, with no speaker visible. In this way we plodded up the hill . . . for about 2 hours or more ending with a long stretch of straightforward mounting, not very steep, but most uninteresting . . . we were completely in the dark . . . at length we reached the top of the first peak, overlooking the little dark blue lake . . . & here we stopped & left the ponies under the shelter of a rock, as the last bit of climbing was too steep for them.

The ground is all tumbled & broken into masses of rock near the top, & must be a very pretty foreground on a clear day. From this point we stood & looked over the sharp edge of rock into the old crater, now partly filled by the little lake. At first it was too foggy to see anything – the clouds lay low on the lake, so that we cd. see nothing past the actual rock on which we were standing, all the rest being lost in mist, & looking very much like the inside of a saucepan with the steam rising out it. But as we were looking, the clouds rolled away for a few minutes, & we just got a peep of the lake. It was lovely, almost a prettier effect than on a clear day ... from this place, we ought to have seen for miles on every side, but I suppose we were not the first tourists who had had the same bad luck, so we tried not to grumble, & held on our way to the top.

The top peak was reached by a little, almost invisible path winding through the clumps of rock, & once on the highest point, we sat down to rest, & munch away at our stodgy cake & sandwiches. There was no view of course, past our own red petticoats grouped one above the other on the cairn of loose stones that formed the pinnacle of the mountain. After munching for some time, we made an effort to get some water, & Pugh took us into a little stone hut close at hand (rather in the bothy style, only not so large, nearly), where travellers cd. sleep who came to see the sunrise. It was a most wretched place of only stone, & dripping wet. For my own part, I wd. much prefer taking my luck on the ground outside than being shut into this little hole with water dripping from the roof. There was a little path leading from this hut which was said to lead to a spring. Pugh went to see but found it dry. How it contrived to be dry after the rains of the last summer no-one knows, but so it was, & we had to begin our journey down the hill without finding the water. We tripped down the hill considerably faster than we had come up, & found the ponies where we had left them, tied under a rock. *(5th September 1860)*

By now their holiday is ending. Their last day is spent buying Welsh gifts to take home and feeling low and sad in spirits. They come 'upon three small children walking close together like little soldiers, & looking just like a quiz upon ourselves, only one of them had a great black bottle, almost as much as she could carry, & looking very suspicious'. When it is time to leave they do so in style for 'the group of small boys who had shared in the scuffle for half pennies were all perched up on the wall to see the last of us . . . .they strained their short necks looking up at that height till the horn sounded, & the coach rattled off'. They are of course, being such a 'larky' party, incapable of keeping up their low spirits and they end up:

. . . by being particularly merry all the coach journey, just because we had firmly expected to be quite the reverse. We kept up our spirits at the beginning with fragments of the stodgy 'Dolgelly cake' being administered in small quantities as we felt the need of need it. It was most edifying to see a little bit timidly broken off the store in the handbag by some poor, dejected member, who evidently needed creature comfort to help her on, & then surreptitiously conveyed to her mouth in what she fancied a quiet, unobtrusive moment. Of course the others were all far too dodgy to let this mild deceptiveness pass unnoticed, having probably been up to the same trick themselves not five minutes before, and the poor wretch was instantly assailed on all sides by the strong minded ones who had not erred so lately. "Oh, how can you! Hardly done breakfast! Nasty, sticky cake!" & so on, they only growing charitable on the point when they had also acted little Jack Horner, & then they were all quick enough to discover that it was nonsense to talk of breakfast. It had been a perfect farce, and besides they had been in far too great a hurry to think of eating, even if the chops had been done, which they were not by any means! We managed to pass the morning merrily enough with one thing & another, learning the verses of some comic songs of which nobody knew the tunes, & purporting to shout them all in chorus next time we met. Then we began to consider the probable expense of a riding tour through different parts of Wales, imagining the present party starting with a sufficient number of ponies & one break to do it comfortably, & calculating what a month at that rate wd. cost. We built our castles in the air very carefully, considering all the items, & found it would be quite feasible, & we all agreed most delightful, but of course not the smallest use to think about, as something always overturns long made schemes, so there our castle remains, up in the air, where we first built it! *(8 September 1860)*

Frederica Rouse Boughton did in fact go back to Wales on two more occasions, by which time she was a wife and mother, but her plan to tour the whole of Wales remained, as she thought it would, as a castle in the air. Yet this one diary of a short intense holiday in which she had 'never had a merrier time' remained in her memory for many years to come. Nearly a hundred and fifty years later her illustrated diary still gives a vivid picture of a group of lively young people having a wonderful time in an exciting landscape with a hospitable people – and makes a fitting end to the adventures of these early lady travellers to Wales.

Afterword

There is no doubt that, between 1795, when Sarah Wilmot and Frances Crewe travelled to Wales, and 1860, when Frederica Rouse Boughton spent her happy fortnight there, conditions for the traveller had improved enormously. This can be seen, for example, in the way that many of the traditional inns improved, as well as in the building of new inns and hotels. Roads too improved, and bridges such as the Menai Bridge made even the remoter parts of Wales accessible. Seaside resorts such as Tenby and Aberystwyth developed, as sea bathing became more and more popular, into resorts for the genteel traveller who would expect both clean lodgings and good food.

Yet alongside these improvements, much of what these diarists experienced has been lost or has virtually disappeared as part of the day-to-day experience of the rural Welsh: the practice of penillion singing, for example, that Frances Crewe observed, has now all but died out as a spontaneous, pub-culture entity – although it lives on in a different form in Eisteddfod competitions; whilst the Welsh harper, a constant, it seems, in the inns that the travellers stayed in, has been replaced by piped music. Nor, sadly, does the thirsty climber of today find a shop selling ginger beer on Castell Dinas Brân!

Yet despite these losses, much remains virtually unchanged since the days when the diarists, in their long, voluminous skirts, floppy hats and heavy boots, their sketch books at the ready, stepped out of their coaches to make a hasty sketch. The ruins have been tidied up; the ivy and the idiosyncratic guides have gone; but their magic and mystery remains. The eccentric owners of great houses now only live on in legend, but their houses remain, even if only as ruins, and these days the public are allowed into many of them.

As for the industry, much of it, new and exciting when the diarists travelled, has in the short space of a hundred years or so, become industrial history, much of that now overgrown in the way that the ruined abbeys and castles once were. But even here, some things remain. The Menai Bridge, probably the industrial wonder that most excited the tourists then, still excites the visitor today; whilst travelling over the Pontcysyllte aqueduct is still a dizzying and vertigo-inducing experience.

And as well as the diaries, the few paintings that have survived also help to paint a visual picture of Wales at the time. Whilst these artists cannot compare with many of the Welsh painters of the period, they nevertheless remain as delightful cameos of happy days spent wandering round ruins, invading Welsh farm houses, or climbing mountains in long red petticoats.

And so, as the diarists say, 'finis' to these spirited, enthusiastic and observant lady travellers of two hundred or so years ago. Although travelling for pleasure today is made easier by good maps, detailed guide books, tourist information centres and the internet, this book might still help today's 'larky' and adventurous travellers to rediscover, in the company of these lively women, the Welsh Tour. Those who do will find the paradise that can, at least in parts, still be found in the grandeur of north Wales and the gentler beauties of the south.

Notes

The Discovery

1 Jinny Jenks' diary is at *http://www.gtj.org.uk/en/item1/5698.*

Chapter 2: The Inquisitive Travellers

1 Parliamentary Archives, Houses of Parliament, HL/PB/1/1792/32G3n69, an Act to dissolve the marriage of John Wilmot, Esquire, with Fanny Sainthill his now wife, and to enable him to marry again; and for other purposes therein mentioned.
2 It has not been possible to discover the exact dates for Sarah's life, but she is probably the Sarah Haslem, daughter of Anthony Haslem, who was baptised on 12th March 1755 (Derbyshire Record Office and Derby Diocesan Record Office, M112 vol. 3). Sarah's will, listed in the Will Registers of the Prerogative Court of Canterbury, is dated 1st July 1831, PROB 11/1788, thus making her about 76 when she died. John was born on 14th May 1749 and died on 26th June 1815, in his sixty-seventh year.
3 Guildhall Library, London, MS 6667/14. The family tree supplied by Michael Wilmot does not, sadly, give details of these children other than their names.

Chapter 6: The Honeymoon Diarist

1 Dorset Record Office, KW 141, Indenture of 21.6.1837.
2 Dorset Record Office, R/397/1875/90, Will of Elizabeth Bower and KW 533, codicil to her will.

Sources used

Malcolm Andrews, *The search for the picturesque: landscape aesthetics and tourism in Britain, 1760 – 1800* (Aldershot, 1989)

David Barnes, *The companion guide to Wales* (Woodbridge, 2005)

Elisabeth Beazley and Peter Howell, *The companion guide to North Wales* (London, 1975)

Edmund Burke, *A philosophical enquiry into the origin of our ideas of the sublime and beautiful 1759, edited with an introduction and notes by J. T. Boulton* (London, 1958)

Giraldus Cambrensis, *The journey through Wales and the description of Wales, translated from the Latin with an introduction by Lewis Thorpe* (London, 1978)

E. A. Davies, *A gazetteer of Welsh place names* (Cardiff, 1967)

John Davies, *The making of Wales* (Stroud, 1996)

Brian Dolan, *Ladies of the Grand Tour* (London, 2001)

John Evans, 'Nathaniel Wells of Piercefield and St Kitts: from slave to sheriff', *The Monmouthshire Antiquary*, XVIII (2002) 91–105

Robin Gard (ed.), *The observant traveller: diaries of travel in England, Wales and Scotland in the county record offices of England and Wales* (London, 1989)

William Gilpin, *Observations on the river Wye and several parts of South Wales, &c. relative chiefly to picturesque beauty, made in the summer of the year 1770* (London, 1789)

Gillian Glegg, *Clapham's past* (London 1998)

Richard Haslam, *Powys* (London, 1979)

Peter Howell and Elisabeth Beazley, *The companion guide to South Wales* (London, 1977)

Edward Hubbard, *Clwyd* (London, 1986)

Elizabeth Inglis-Jones, *Peacocks in paradise* (Llandysul, 2001)

Keith Kissack, *The river Wye* (Lavenham, 1978)

Peter Lord, *The visual culture of Wales volume 2, imaging the nation* (Cardiff, 2000)

H. C. G. Matthew and Brian Harrison eds., *Oxford dictionary of national biography from the earliest times to the year 2000* (Oxford, 2004)

Elizabeth Mavor, *The ladies of Llangollen: a study in romantic friendship* (London, 2001)

Esther Moir, *The discovery of Britain, the English tourists 1540 – 1840* (London, 1964)

Prys Morgan ed., *The Tempus history of Wales 25,000 B.C. – A. D. 2000.* (Stroud, 2001)

Jan Morris, *The matter of Wales – epic views of a small country* (Oxford, 1984)

Tony Newbery, *Travelling for pleasure* (Llandysul, 1994)

John Newman, *Gwent/Monmouthshire* (London, 2000)

John Newman, *Glamorgan* (London, 1995)

Mike Parker and Paul Whitfield, *The Rough Guide to Wales* (London, 2000)

Brenda Parry, *Aunt Emily's Caerynwch journals* (unpublished 1961)

Thomas Pennant, *A tour in Wales, MDCCLXXIII* (London 1778)

J. A. R. Pimlott, *The Englishman's holiday* (Hassocks 1947)

John A. Smith, *A compilation of a parish and its people* (unpublished, no date)

Herbert Williams, *Stage coaches in Wales* (Barry, 1977)

Alyson Wilson ed., *The buildings of Clapham* (London, 2000)

Peter Wortsman (trans), Adelbert von Chamisso, *Peter Schlemiel, the man who sold his shadow* (New York, 2003)

Further reading – a brief list of published journeys by women

Margaret Fountaine, *Love among the butterflies, travels and adventures of a victorian lady* (Collins, 1980)

Catherine Hutton, 'Letters on journeys to Wales' *Monthly Magazine*, March 1816 onwards

Samuel Johnson, *Dr Johnson and Mrs Thrale's tour in North Wales 1774, with an introduction and notes by Adrian Bristow* (Wrexham, 1995)

Mrs Mary Morgan, *A Tour to Milford Haven, in the year 1791* (London, 1795)

Jane Robinson, *Unsuitable for ladies, an anthology of women travellers* (Oxford, 1994)

Mrs Elizabeth Selwyn, *Journal of excursions through the most interesting parts of England, Wales and Scotland, during the summers and autumns of 1819, 1820, 1821, 1822 and 1823* (London, 1824)

Catherine Sinclair, *Hill and valley, or hours in England and Wales 1833* (1st edition, New York, 1838)

Elizabeth Spence, *Summer excursions through parts of Oxfordshire, Gloucestershire, Warwickshire, Staffordshire, Herefordshire, Derbyshire, and South Wales, 1768-1832, 2nd edition, 2 vols* (London, 1809)

Louisa A Twamley, *The annual of British landscape scenery; an autumn ramble on the Wye* (London, 1839)

Margaret Willy, *Three women diarists: Celia Fiennes, Dorothy Wordsworth, Katherine Mansfield* (London, 1964)

Appendix 1

The diaries and their locations

Chapter 1:
Bedfordshire and Luton Archives and Record Service (BLARS)
Ann Bletchley's diary in the form of a letter, 1812 with no other date than October, SY 49.

Caernarfon Record Office
Harriet Alderson's 'Journal of a tour from Aston to Beaumaris in September 1818', XM/2600.

Cardiff Libraries and Information Service
Judith Beecroft: 'Excursion to north Wales, 1827', Ms2.325. (Note: this diary is referenced as being by a Norwich man, but internal evidence shows it to be by a Norwich widow.)
Annie Lewis Hodgson: 'Account of a tour of England and Wales, 1855', Ms3.248.
Charlotte Jane Skinner: 'Sketch book, done in the summer of 1808', Ms3.295.
Esther Williams: 'Journal of a trip to Glamorganshire, 1836', Ms1.521.

Gloucestershire Archives
Mary Russell: 'Tour from Gloucestershire into south Wales 1804', D388/F2.

Llyfrgell Genedlaethol Cymru – National Library of Wales
Ann Atherton: 'Tour of north Wales and Cardiganshire, 1825', 20366B.

Shropshire Archives
Louisa Charlotte Kenyon's diary of a trip to north Wales, 1839, 549/286.

Worcestershire Record Office
Ann Porter: 'Journal of a tour down the Wye & through south Wales, August 17 to September 25, 1824', BA 3940 Parcel 65 (ii) 705: 262.

Chapter 2:
British Library
Frances Anne Crewe, Welsh travel diary for 1795, Add 37926.

Llyfrgell, Amgueddfa Cymru – Library, National Museum, Wales
Sarah Anne Wilmot: 'Journal from 1792–1810', Acc.No.179554. This includes a Welsh journey in 1795 and another in 1802. The 1802 diary: 'Sarah Anne Wilmot's visit to Gloucestershire, Monmouthshire and the Vale of Glamorgan' can also be seen at: *www.gtj.org.uk/en/item6/19025.*

Wigan Archive Services, WLCT
Sarah Haslam: Welsh travel journal 1802, MS969 EHC177.

Chapter 3:
Essex Record Office
Millicent Bant's diary of a north Wales visit 1806, D/DFr F2; and diary of south Wales visits 1808 and 1812, D/DFr F4.

Chapter 4:
Gloucestershire Archives
Mary Anne Hibbert's diary for 1816, D1799 F320.
Mary Anne Hibbert: 'Journal of a tour on the Wye & from Bath to Cheshire July 1823', D1799 F322.
Mary Anne Hibbert's diary for 1849, 1850, 1851, D1799 F334.
Mary Ann Hibbert's diary for 1856, D1799 F337.
Sarah Hibbert, 'Trip through parts of England, & Wye Tour', D1799 F346.

Chapter 5:
Hampshire Record Office
Margaret Martineau, travel diary for 1824, 83M93/21, with biographical notes being extracted from the description in 83M93.

Chapter 6:
Dorset History Centre
Elizabeth Bower: travel diary for 1837, D/BOW:KW209.

Chapter 7:
Bedfordshire and Luton Archives and Record Service
Frederica Rouse Boughton's diary for 1860 includes Our Fortnight in Wales, OR 2244/5a.

A list of the most interesting of the diaries seen and transcribed:

Bodleian Library, Oxford
Fanny Symonds: 'Journal of a holiday to the Isle of Wight c. 1837' Ms Don e 143.

Cambridgeshire County Record Office
Lady Philadelphia Cotton: 'Tour through north Wales, 1819', Ms 588DR/F48.

Cambridge University Library
Mrs West: travel diary for north Wales 1810, MS Add.738.

Cardiff Libraries and Information Service
A lady: 'Diary of a driving tour of north Wales in the months of July and August 1811', Ms1.405.
Miss Dovaston: 'A Few Remarks on a Journey to Shropshire and north Wales 1846', MS.3.149.

Centre for Kentish Studies – depositor Maidstone Museum
Mary Coare: 'Diary of a tour in the West Country and Wales c 1830', U1823/8 Z4.

County Record Office, Cambridge
Lady Philadelphia Cotton: 'Tour through north Wales 1819', 588DR/F48.

Denbighshire Record Office
Sarah Brinkley: 'Journal of a tour from Dublin via Holyhead and north Wales into England 1822', DD/PR/133.

Hull University Archives
Lady Sykes: 'Journal of a tour in Wales, by Lady Sykes, 1796. Transcribed by Catharine Sherwood, June-July 1918. Held as part of the Sykes of Sledmere family and estate archives', DDSY3/10/11.

Leicestershire, Leicester and Rutland Record Office
Eliza Spurrett: 'Journal of a Tour in north Wales 1825', ROLLR 7D54/2/1
Eliza Spurrett: 'Journal, including a Tour in north Wales 1841', ROLLR 7D54/2/3

Llyfrgell, Amgueddfa Cymru – National Museum Wales, Library
Elisabeth Winnington: 'Tour into north Wales September 1804', Acc. No. 147085.

Llyfrgell Genedlaethol Cymru – National Library of Wales
Mary Anne Eade: 'Tour of north Wales and Ireland 1802', NLW MS 22190B.
Jinny Jenks: 'Tour of north Wales 1772', NLW MS 22753B.
Mrs William Shepherd (Frances Nicholson): 'Tour of north Wales 1790', NLW MS 15190C.
Sophia Ward: 'Tour from England to south Wales and south-west England 1791', NLW MS 19758A.
Hannah Wood: 'Sketches in north Wales 1842, Drawing volume 26' (this includes some diary notes).

Shropshire Archives
Louisa Charlotte Kenyon: 'Tour through part of north Wales 1803', 549/212.
Louisa Charlotte Kenyon: 'Journal of a tour in south Wales 1837', 549/285.
Louisa Charlotte Kenyon: 'Journal of tour to north Wales 1839', 549/286.
Katherine Plymley: 'Journey to Anglesey 1792', 567/5/5/1/1.

Katherine Plymley: 'Journey to Tenby and Voyage to Penzance 1802', 567/5/5/1/20.

Katherine Plymley: 'Journey to Parkgate and Pistyll Rhaiadr 1814', 567/5/5/1/30.

Somerset Record and Archive Service
Elizabeth Ernst: 'Journey to Wales 1 – 17 October 1826', DD\SWD/10/7.

Wigan Archives Service, WLCT
Lucy Wright: 'A tour of England and Wales 1806', M842 EHC 73.

Wiltshire and Swindon Record Office
Charlotte Mary Hobhouse: 'Journal kept whilst touring north Wales 1855', 112/2/7.

Worcestershire Record Office
Martha Porter: 'Journal of a tour down the Wye & through south Wales 1824', BA 3940 Parcel 64 (ii) 705:262.
Phoebe Porter: 'Journal of a tour through south Wales 1824', BA 3940 Parcel 68 (i) 705: 262.
Hannah Williams: 'Journey through Shropshire, Wales, Ireland & Lancashire 1831, 899:866/9522.

Appendix 2

Gazetteer of place-names and inns

The places listed below appear in bold on their first mention in the book. For more information on which to base a tour see The Companion Guide to Wales by David Barnes. The National Trust and Cadw also publish full details of their properties, together with opening times and facilities available. Many of the sites mentioned also have websites.

The place-names

Aber, Gwynedd	Abbreviation for Abergwyngregyn, Gwynedd
Aberdulais, Neath Port Talbot	National Trust
Abergavenny, Monmouthshire	Small market town
Aberystwyth, Ceredigion	Seaside and University town, castle in care of local authority
Acton Park, Wrexham	Demolished in 1954
Anglesey, Isle of	Island off the coast of north Wales
Aran Benllyn, Gwynedd	2,901 ft
Bala, Gwynedd	Famous for its lake. See Llyn Tegid
Bangor, Gwynedd	Cathedral, university town
Barmouth, Gwynedd	Resort at mouth of Mawddach estuary
Baron Hill, Isle of Anglesey	Private hands
Beaumaris, Isle of Anglesey	Small town on Menai Strait, castle (Cadw)
Beddgelert, Gwynedd	Village famed for legend of the dog Gelert
Benarth Hall, Gwynedd	Private hands
Bersham Ironworks, Wrexham	Heritage Centre and Museum complex
Berw, Pontypridd, Rhondda, Cynon, Taff	Waterfall much affected by blasting but still accessible
Betws-y-Coed, Conwy	Popular walking centre
Brecon, Powys	Market town, cathedral
Briton Ferry, Neath Port Talbot	Small historic industrial town
Brynffynnon, Dolgellau, Gwynedd	Private hands
Buckstone, Gloucestershire	On edge of Staunton village
Builth Wells, Powys	Riverside town with arts centre
Cadair Idris, Gwynedd	2,930 ft
Caerleon, Newport	Amphitheatre (Cadw) also Legionary Museum
Caernarfon, Gwynedd	Small town on Menai Strait, castle (Cadw)
Caerphilly Castle, Caerphilly	Cadw
Caerwent, Monmouthshire	Roman remains (Cadw)
Caerynwch, Gwynedd	Private hands
Caldey Island, Pembrokeshire	Island and abbey open when weather permits

Caldicot Castle, Monmouthshire	Country Park
Cambrian Pottery, Swansea	Closed 1870
Capel Curig, Conwy	Centre for mountain-climbers and hill-walkers
Cardiff	Capital; castle (open) owned by Cardiff City
Cardigan, Ceredigion	Market town on Teifi estuary
Carew Castle, Pembrokeshire	National Park, SSSI, open to the public
Carew Cross, Pembrokeshire	Cadw
Carmarthen, Carmarthenshire	Commercial town, castle
Carreg Cennen Castle, Carmarthenshire	Cadw
Castell Malgwyn, Pembrokeshire	Now a hotel
Cenarth, Ceredigion	Salmon leap, National Coracle Centre
Cernioge, Conwy	Private hands
Charlton House, Kent	Metropolitan Borough of Greenwich
Chepstow, Monmouthshire	Small border town, castle (Cadw)
Chirk Castle, Wrexham	National Trust
Cilgerran Castle, Pembrokeshire	Cadw
Clytha Castle, Monmouthshire	Landmark Trust
Coldbrook House, Monmouthshire	Demolished in 1954
Coldwell Rocks, Gloucestershire	One of the official Wye tour viewpoints
Conwy, Conwy	Castle and town walls (Cadw)
Corwen, Denbighshire	Heart of Glyndŵr country
Cowbridge, Vale of Glamorgan	Small country town
Crewe Hall, Cheshire	Now a hotel
Criccieth, Gwynedd	Small coastal town, castle (Cadw)
Crickhowell, Powys	Small country town on Usk
Cynfal Falls, Gwynedd	Waterfall near village of Llan Ffestiniog
Denbigh, Denbighshire	Small market town, castle (Cadw)
Devil's Bridge, Ceredigion	Privately owned, open to the public
Dinas Brân, Denbighshire	Hill fort and medieval castle
Dinefwr Castle, Carmarthenshire	National Trust
Dolgellau, Gwynedd	Small town at the foot of Cadair Idris
Downton Hall, Shropshire	Private hands
Dryslwyn Castle, Carmarthenshire	Cadw
Dunraven Castle, Bridgend	Heritage Coast Centre
Edwinsford, Carmarthenshire	Derelict
Erddig, Wrexham	National Trust
Ewenni Priory, Vale of Glamorgan	Cadw
Fishguard, Pembrokeshire	Harbour and ferry to Ireland
Fontmell Parva, Dorset	Privately owned
Gloddaeth, Conwy	Independent secondary school
Glyndyfrdwy vale, Denbighshire	Valley between Llangollen and Corwen
Glyngarth, Isle of Anglesey	Now apartments
Glynhir, Carmarthenshire	Venue for residential courses
Gnoll, Neath Port Talbot	Country Park

Golden Grove, Carmarthenshire	Country Park
Goodrich Castle, Herefordshire	English Heritage
Gower Peninsula, Swansea	AONB
Gwydir Castle, Conwy	Private hands, open to the public
Hafod, Ceredigion	House demolished; grounds managed by the Forestry Commission
Hare Hill, Cheshire	National Trust
Harlech, Gwynedd	Small town near coast, castle (Cadw)
Haverfordwest, Pembrokeshire	On western Cleddau
Hay-on-Wye, Powys	Small country town, literary festival
Holyhead, Isle of Anglesey	Port with busy ferry service to Ireland
Holywell Chapel, Flintshire	Cadw
Kenfig Pool, Bridgend	Nature reserve
Kymin, Monmouthshire	National Trust
Kidwelly Castle, Carmarthenshire	Cadw
Lampeter College, Ceredigion	University of Wales, Lampeter
Laugharne, Carmarthenshire	Coastal village with castle (Cadw)
Llanberis, Gwynedd	Small town popular with walkers
Llanberis Pass, Gwynedd	One of the most dramatic Welsh passes
Llandaf, Cardiff	Cardiff's cathedral
Llandeilo, Carmarthenshire	Small market town
Llandovery, Carmarthenshire	Small market town
Llandrindod Wells, Powys	Pump room now a café, spa water available
Llandudno, Conwy	Seaside town and resort
Llanegryn, Gwynedd	Small village near coast
Llanfair Caereinion, Powys	Welshpool & Llanfair Light Railway
Llangollen, Denbighshire	Small town, International Eisteddfod
Llangybi Castle, Monmouthshire	Private hands
Llanidloes, Powys	Small market town
Llanrhaeadr, Denbighshire	Some of finest stained glass in Wales
Llanrwst, Conwy	Small market town
Llansteffan Castle, Carmarthenshire	Cadw
Llanthony Priory, Monmouthshire	Cadw
Llantrisant, Rhondda Cynon Taff	Hilltop village
Llantrithyd, Vale of Glamorgan	A ruin
Llantwit Major, Vale of Glamorgan	Small town on heritage coast
Lleweni Hall, Denbighshire	Only outbuildings left, private hands
Llwyngwril, Gwynedd	Small coastal village
Llyn Cwellyn, Gwynedd	Between Beddgelert and Caernarfon
Llyn Idwal, Gwynedd	Lake in Cwm Idwal nature reserve
Llyn Peninsula, Gwynedd	Most westerly part of north Wales
Llyn Tegid, Gwynedd	Largest natural freshwater lake in Wales
Machynlleth, Powys	Market town, Museum Modern Art
Maenan Abbey, Conwy	Hotel now stands on site
Maesteg Iron Works, Bridgend	Former mining valley town

Manorbier Castle, Pembrokeshire	Privately owned, open to the public
Margam, Neath Port Talbot	Country Park
Menai Bridge	Road bridge from mainland to Anglesey
Menai Strait, Isle of Anglesey	Strait between mainland and Anglesey
Merthyr Tydfil, Merthyr Tydfil	Former iron works, commercial town
Middleton Hall, Carmarthenshire	National Botanic Garden of Wales
Monmouth, Monmouthshire	Small county town, castle (Cadw)
Montgomery, Powys	Small country town, castle (Cadw)
Nannau, Gwynedd	Virtually derelict, in private hands
Nant Ffrancon, Gwynedd	Glaciated valley near Cwm Idwal
Nant Gwynant, Gwynedd	Valley between Beddgelert and Snowdon
Neath, Neath Port Talbot	Large urban centre, castle (Cadw)
Newcastle Emlyn, Carmarthenshire	Open access to ruins of castle
Newport, Newport	Port, commercial centre, castle (Cadw)
Ogwen Pool, Gwynedd	Popular lake in north Wales
Old Beaupre Castle, Vale of Glamorgan	Cadw
Orielton, Pembrokeshire	Owned by Field Studies Council since 1963; hosts 3,500 students each year on residential fieldwork.
Parys Mountain, Isle of Anglesey	Heritage Trail available
Pembroke, Pembrokeshire	Small town, castle open to the public
Penmaenmawr, Conwy	Headland on north Wales coast
Penrhyn Castle, Gwynedd	National Trust
Penrhyn Slate Quarries, Gwynedd	Owned by McAlpine's
Penrice Castle, Swansea	Private hands
Picton Castle, Pembrokeshire	Picton Castle Trust, open to the public
Piercefield, Monmouthshire	Private hands
Pistyll Cain, Gwynedd	150 ft waterfall in Coed y Brenin forest
Plas Mawr House, Conwy	Cadw
Plas Newydd, Isle of Anglesey	National Trust
Plas Newydd, Llangollen, Denbighshire	Denbighshire Council, open to the public
Pont Aberglaslyn, Gwynedd	Famous beauty spot, seventeenth-century bridge
Pontcysyllte Aqueduct, Wrexham	Pedestrian access on the towpath
Pont-nedd-fechan, Neath Port Talbot	Village on edge of Brecons
Pontypridd, Rhondda Cynon Taff	Gateway to Rhondda
Portmadoc, Gwynedd	Mouth of the Glaslyn river
Powis Castle, Powys	National Trust
Precipice Walk, Gwynedd	Three-mile walk with stunning views, within the Nannau estate, open with permission of the Vaughan family, looked after by Snowdonia National Park
Raglan Castle, Monmouthshire	Cadw
Rhaeadr Ddu, Gwynedd	National Trust
Rhaeadr Mawddach, Gwynedd	60 ft waterfall in Coed y Brenin forest

Rhayader, Powys	Small market town
Rivals, Gwynedd	On the Llyn Peninsula
Ross-on-Wye, Herefordshire	Small market town
Ruthin, Denbighshire	Small market town, castle now a hotel
St. Asaph, Denbighshire	Smallest Welsh cathedral
St. Briavels, Gloucestershire	Castle now a youth hostel
St. Brides Major, Vale of Glamorgan	Village near south Wales Heritage coast
St. David's, Pembrokeshire	Cathedral city, Bishop's Palace (Cadw)
St. Dogmaels Abbey, Ceredigion	Cadw
St. Donat's, Vale of Glamorgan	Atlantic College, Arts Centre
St. Dyfnog's Well, Denbighshire	A short walk from the churchyard
St. Govan's, Pembrokeshire	St. Govan's cell and two holy wells
Skirrid Fawr, Monmouthshire	National Trust
Snowdon, Gwynedd	3650 ft, highest Welsh mountain
Stack Rocks, Pembrokeshire	SSSI, open to the public
Stackpole Court, Pembrokeshire	National Trust
Sugarloaf, Monmouthshire	National Trust
Swallow Falls, Gwynedd	Popular beauty spot near Betws-y-Coed
Swansea, Swansea	University town
Symonds Yat, Herefordshire	Viewpoint and visitor centre
Symondsbury, Dorset	Quiet little village
Taff's Well, Cardiff	Once a mineral well, now disused
Taliaris, Carmarthenshire	Venue for residential courses
Tallyllyn, Gwynedd	Lake to the south of Cadair Idris
Tan y Bwlch, Gwynedd	Field study centre, Snowdonia National Park
Tenby, Pembrokeshire	Coastal town and resort
Tintern Abbey, Monmouthshire	Cadw
Torrent Walk, Gwynedd	2.5-mile walk, originally laid out by Baron Richards of Caerynwch
Trecastle, Powys	Norman motte
Tredegar House, Newport	Newport City Council, open to the public
Tregaron, Ceredigion	Market town in foothills of Cambrians
Tremadoc, Gwynedd	Small planned town
Tywyn, Gwynedd	Tallyllyn narrow gauge railway
Usk, Monmouthshire	Castle in private hands open to the public
Vale of Glamorgan, Vale of Glamorgan	Area of coast with rural hinterland
Vale of Llangollen, Denbigh	Valley between Llangollen and Corwen
Vale of Neath, Neath Port Talbot	Valley from Neath to Pont-nedd-Fechan
Valle Crucis, Denbighshire	Cadw
Water Break Its Neck, Powys	Dramatic waterfall in Warren woods
Welshpool, Powys	Small market town on Welsh border
Wrexham, Wrexham	Commercial centre
Wyndcliff, Monmouthshire	365 steps lead to Eagle's Nest viewpoint

The inns

Anchor, Tintern, Monmouthshire	Still exists
Angel, Abergavenny, Monmouthshire	Still exists
Bear, Cowbridge, Vale of Glamorgan	Still exists
Beaufort Arms, Chepstow, Monmouthshire	Still exists
Beaufort Arms, Monmouth, Monmouthshire	Now apartments, shops
Black Lion, Cardigan, Ceredigion	Still exists
Caernarfon Hotel, Caernarfon	No information
Cann Office, near Welshpool, Powys	Still exists
Cardiff Arms, Cardiff, Cardiff	No information
Castle, Brecon, Powys	Still exists
Castle, Haverfordwest, Pembrokeshire	Still exists
Castle, St. Briavels	Now a Youth Hostel
Coburg, Tenby, Pembrokeshire	Now apartments, shops
Ferry House, Bangor, Gwynedd	No information
George, St Briavels, Gloucestershire	Still exists
Green Dragon, Pembroke, Pembrokeshire	Now the Natwest bank
Hafod Arms, Devil's Bridge, Ceredigion	Still exists
Hand, Llangollen, Denbighshire	Still exists
King's Head, Builth Wells, Powys	Now car park, Lamb inn
King's Head, Llangollen, Denbighshire	Now the Royal
Mackworth Arms, Swansea, Swansea	Post office on site
New Bridge Arms, Caernarfon, Gwynedd	No information
New Ivy Bush, Carmarthen, Carmarthenshire	Now Ivy Bush Royal
Oakeley Arms, Tan y Bwlch, Gwynedd	Still exists
Penrhyn Arms, Bangor, Gwynedd	Demolished
Princes Feathers, Tavernspite, Pembrokeshire	Closed 1930s
Pyle Inn, Pyle, Bridgend	Demolished c.1960
Queen's Hotel, Llandudno, Gwynedd	Still exists
Royal Hotel, Capel Curig, Conwy	Now Mountain Centre
Royal Oak, Rhayader, Powys	Still exists
Royal Victoria Hotel, Llanberis, Gwynedd	Still exists
Three Salmons, Usk, Monmouthshire	Still exists
White Lion, Conwy, Gwynedd	Closed
White Lion, Ruthin, Denbighshire	Now Castle hotel
White Lion, Tenby, Pembrokeshire	Now Royal Lion Hotel

Credits for illustrations:

Unless mentioned otherwise, photographs are by the author.

Frederica Rouse Boughton's watercolours © Bedfordshire and Luton Archives and Record Service (BLARS)

Watercolours and sketch by Sarah Wilmot (Haslam) from her Wigan diary © Wigan Archives Service, WLCT

Watercolours of Newport and Monmouth by Sarah Wilmot (Haslam) from her Cardiff diary © National Museum of Wales, Library

Painting: *Pont Aberglaslyn* © David Barnes

Frederica Rouse Boughton as a child © Mr and Mrs Wiggin, Downton Hall

Bersham Ironworks: *Drawing of the West Works* by John Westway Rowe, c. 1790.
© Bersham Heritage Centre, Wrexham Heritage Services

Dolgellau in 1849 © Andrew Richards

Drawing of Welsh Fashions Taken on a Market-Day in Wales 1851 by R. Griffiths © Ceredigion Museum, Aberystwyth

Bathing place in Cardigan Bay near Aberystwyth by J Hassell, 1790s © Ceredigion Museum, Aberystwyth

Drawing Devil's Bridge by David Cox, c.1820, © Ceredigion Museum, Aberystwyth

Photograph: Tredegar House © Newport City Council

Painting: Orielton House, by J P Neale, pre 1809 © Field Studies Council

Photograph: Coracles © National Coracle Centre, Cenarth

Walking Books ....

Visit our website for further information:
www.carreg-gwalch.com

Orders can be placed on our
On-line Shop

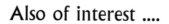